Brÿon

The
Snafu Principle

Lets connect

Ron Hurst

R

Published by Best Seller Publishing, Pasadena, California.
Best Seller Publishing is a registered trademark.

ISBN-13: 978-1519113351
ISBN-10: 1519113358
LCCN:

DISCLAIMER
This publication is designed to provide accurate and authoritative information with regard to the subject matter covered. It is sold with the understanding that the publisher is not engaged in rendering legal, accounting, or other professional advice. If legal advice or other expert assistance is required, the services of a competent professional should be sought. The opinions expressed by the author in this book are not endorsed by Best Seller Publishing and are the sole responsibility of the author rendering the opinion.

Most Best Seller Publishing titles are available at special quantity discounts for bulk purchases for sales promotions, premiums, fundraising, and educational use. Special versions or book excerpts can also be created to fi t specifi c needs.

For more information, please write:
Best Seller Publishing
1346 Walnut Street, #205
Pasadena, CA 91106

Or call 1 (626) 765-9750
Toll Free: 1 (844) 850-3500
Visit us online at: www.BestSellerPublishing.org

Printed in the United States of America.

To Kim, Mitch, and Meg

Thank you for the innumerable opportunities you each have provided me in learning to be a more effective communicator. Through this you have taught me to be a better husband and father.

With love, Ron

Contents

Part 1/The Snafu Principle

CHAPTER ONE

INTRODUCTION

In the 25 years that I've been in industry, I've had the opportunity to work with a number of different organizations. Many of them were leaders in their field. Some were middle of the pack, others were just struggling to survive and make a profit. Regardless of where they were in their market space, one thing remained the same: all of them had challenges with communication. Wherever a company is in its lifecycle—a startup, an entrepreneurial dream, a small fledgling growing business, an established growing business, or one of those staid old economy companies that are slowly transferring into the night (or straight up in decline)—all companies deal with communication challenges.

Miscommunication, under-communication, there are as many ways to describe this phenomenon, as there are ways to communicate. I truly believe these companies have not invested the time in developing communication processes, to upskilling their employees to a point where they can be effective in all aspects of communication. Communicating with peers, customers, employees, and with supervisors—make no mistake—people need to change the way that they approach it.

Many companies don't know how to consistently communicate in order to get results. According to recent research, companies with poor communication skills have higher turnover, increased employee absenteeism rates, poorer customer service, greater numbers of accidents, and lower shareholder value. If this isn't a business case for effective communication—

Communication Woes	
Employee turnover	+17%[1]
Productivity	$26,000 loss per employee[2]
Disengaged employees	68% costing $450–$550B[3]
Accidents attributed to communication	70%[4]
Impact to market value	-29.5%[5]

The cost is astronomical. We're talking tens of hundreds of millions of dollars in lost productivity, not to mention companies that are destroyed over miscommunication and are no longer represented in the statistics. The relational damage alone is tragic.

There have been so many times throughout my career that I've gone to talk to employees about a change process or announce a new initiative that the company's going to do and the first thing I hear out of their mouths is, "That'll never work!" It really is quite remarkable when you hear a comment like that because it's not usually said in a monotone, logical voice. In fact, the delivery makes it quite clear that there's a depth of emotion behind what they're saying. Many employees have been victims of past change processes—they've experienced ways in which the organization has gone in a specific direction and the results have been devastating to them, either professionally or personally (or both).

Perhaps it was something as simple as a supervisor coming to an employee in frustration about his performance, but the supervisor was unable to effectively share his or her thoughts in a constructive way. Instead of communicating in a productive way, the supervisor might have relayed the message in such a way that it cut to the heart of the employee's pride, his ego, and his self-concept. Perhaps he was left a wreck on the job, trying to pick up the pieces, maintain employment, and provide for his family, when he didn't feel complete anymore. It might have led to a vicious cycle—the employee didn't feel like he could make a contribution, so he shut down and put up a defensive barrier. That wall became so strong and deep that it became increasingly difficult for the supervisor, the manager, or other people in the organization to get through to that employee ever again.

This is the reality of failed communication in corporations. If everyone doesn't understand how to effectively communicate with employees, with peers, and with supervisors, they will end up in a place of under-performance.

I dare say that you, the reader of this book, are struggling with exactly the type of challenge that I've just laid out. Let me tell a few stories, and you can see if you find yourself in any of them.

Reflection

1. How is poor communication affecting your company's bottom line?

2. What is your reason for improving your communication effectiveness?

CHAPTER TWO

STORIES OF FAILURE

Graffiti

Several years ago, I had the opportunity to work with a group of manufacturing employees. I walked in early one morning on a maintenance outage day. We had put our plan together the previous day, everything was in order, and things were going well, or so I thought. When I walked into one of our receiving areas, I noticed a skid of product with graffiti written on it. I thought, *that's strange, graffiti in my shop? Nobody does that.*

As I approached this pallet of material, I realized that it wasn't graffiti as much as it was a criticism and challenge of another crew. The night-shift crew had written "FOR A GOOD SCREWING, SEE X SHIFT" all over this particular pallet. I took one look and realized that this was a real challenge. This could undermine the culture of our operation.

I immediately stopped our maintenance outage, grabbed my crew together, and held an impromptu town hall meeting in front of this pallet. I talked to the employees—the same employees to whom this pallet had been delivered on the previous day—about what was going on. They had obviously not put it away, hence the night crew's decision to express its frustration through graffiti. I explained to everyone present the importance of doing his or her job correctly.

As I got into the issue, I spoke passionately about the importance of working together collaboratively. I had each one of those employees listening to every word I said. Eventually I discovered the root cause of the incident: a vendor had delivered this product at the end of the shift when no employees were present and hadn't told anyone. I realized that not only had the day-shift crew NOT caused this situation, but also the night- shift crew had made way too many assumptions.

I had this exact same meeting with the night-shift crew, except the tone of the meeting was quite different. I started out in a level, even tone. I physically received the product and put it away as I held the meeting. By the time I was done talking about the importance of communicating and working together effectively, I was yelling. [I had never yelled at any employee in this company in the previous five years that I'd worked there. This was the first time I'd ever done it and I did it purposefully. I was not angry; I was emphasizing a critical point. By the time I was done, again every one of these employees realized the error that they had made].

As I walked away from the meeting, one of the employees from the crew approached me privately.

"Ron, I need to talk to you about something."

Our conversation went like this:

(Ron) *"What's up?"*

(Employee) *"I was the one who wrote the graffiti on that pallet."* (Ron) *"Really, why'd you do that?"*

(Employee) *"I didn't understand what had happened. I thought they were trying to make us do their job."*

(Ron) *"OK, so what did you learn from this?"*

(Employee) *"Yeah, I need to not make assumptions about communication. I need to actually check with them rather than jump to conclusions and create a problem."*

(Ron) *"It sounds like you learned an important lesson."* (Employee) *"Yeah, I did."*

(Ron) *"Can I count on you to never do that again?"* (Employee) *"Yeah, you got my word."*

(Ron) *"OK, then we're done."*

I know many of you managers are shaking your heads right now and thinking, *Holy cow, you caught the guy red-handed, he confessed, and all you did was ask him never to do it again?* Yes, that's exactly what I did. You know what? That employee continued to work for me for another three years. He was true to his word and never did do it again—he demonstrated integrity, and he actually owned the outcome of his miscommunication.

I firmly believe that the culture of our work team was reinforced through this event. Something that could have literally ripped it apart and caused us to under-perform for the next several years became a defining moment for our team. Because I handled it in such a way as to drive to the root cause, and actually solve it, that miscommunication, that assumption, embedded within an employee's day, never became the land mine that it could have easily become.

Communication is such an important aspect in the life of a manager and the success of a business. It's so important that we figure out how to do it right and hold our employees accountable in an uplifting way that will enable them to succeed moving forward.

Overreaction

I want you to imagine that you have an employee named Pat. I chose that name just because it could be male or female, it doesn't really matter. Pat is an average employee who does a decent job. There's nothing spectacular about Pat: they're around their performance target, sometimes they're below, sometimes they're above—they just do their job. They show up on time, most of the time. They get the job done, most of the time. You have little trouble with them and, overall, Pat's an average employee.

Now let's meet the manager, Taylor. Taylor comes into work one day and observes Pat. Pat unfortunately makes a serious error that puts a number one client's shipment behind schedule. Because of this slip-up, a critical order will not be delivered on time to this important client. It's clear that Pat was responsible. Taylor, not being particularly skilled in how to provide communication in the form of feedback, goes to Pat and tears a strip off them. "Why the heck did you do that? Don't you understand the implications of what you've just done? You've just cost us a very important contract. We're going to be late and it's going to cost us all kinds of money. How could you be so careless?"

Now let's take a quick look at Pat. As noted, Pat is your average employee, not particularly sophisticated, not particularly well-educated, just a noble person trying to provide for their family. They do a good job for an honest day's wage. They don't have the sophistication to be able to handle the kind of feedback that's just been given to them. They don't have the thick skin that it takes to manage that kind of withering criticism. What happens to Pat when they receive this particular barrage? Most likely what's going to happen is that they're going to be absolutely devastated. They're going to begin to wonder whether their job is secure—**whether they will have a job tomorrow.** They'll start to wonder about whether they can provide for their family or whether they'll be able to maintain their household. If you think about the fact that most American families are one paycheck away from financial ruin, this is a fairly serious situation for Pat. According to a recent *Wall Street Journal* article, 55 percent of US households do not have enough liquid cash savings to replace one month's wages.[6]

That's the end of day one. Taylor tears the strip off Pat. Day two, day three, day four—what does Taylor do when they're out in the facility and they come across Pat the employee? Chances are Taylor is a much better manager than that first event gives him credit for and he's going to feel a little bit guilty. Taylor will realize that he overreacted, realize he lost control and that his approach to this problem was probably way overdone. The challenge is that most supervisors and managers don't have the ability to go back and say, "I'm sorry." That part of the communication puzzle has not been fully explained to them, the importance of actually apologizing and allowing the employee to heal.

Rather than deal with the problem, what does Taylor do? Most likely when he sees Pat at the end of the aisle, Taylor's going to make a slight turn and keep going, just to avoid the situation. In Taylor's mind, it's easier to avoid Pat rather than deal with the discomfort and the awkwardness of actually engaging that employee because he knows he was wrong.

Here you have a situation, a devastated employee who's afraid for their job and afraid for their future. You have a manager who feels guilty because he's done something kind of over the edge and doesn't know quite how to deal with it.

Come back to Pat with me for a minute. What do you think is going on in Pat's mind when Taylor's making a concerted effort to avoid them? Chances are Pat sees Taylor taking a turn, avoiding going down the aisle, and so Pat thinks, *Uh-oh, he's avoiding me. What's that about?*

Now Pat is beginning to feel self-conscious. Pat thinks, *What am I doing wrong today? Am I doing my job well?* Pat will start to focus more on the worry and the anxiety of why Taylor isn't engaging with them rather than focusing on doing the job well. What do you think is going to happen when Pat stops focusing on the job and starts focusing inward? Yeah, unfortunately Pat makes another mistake. Taylor's got a bigger problem now. Because the situation wasn't reconciled in the first place, a bigger problem appears. How does Taylor handle this one? You guessed it—this is going to get ugly, fast.

You see where I'm going here, folks? The challenge is that if you start to go down this road, and you don't deal with people and communicate in an effective way that maintains dignity and respect and gives people the opportunity to correct their mistakes upfront, things will get ugly fast. I can only imagine that in this particular situation, Pat will end up on the unemployment line. Why? All because Pat made a mistake. That's tragic, absolutely tragic that such a thing could ever happen in a business.

Before you say, "Well, that would never happen here," I want you to just change the names and replace it with somebody that you have communicated ineffectively with. Now tell me that it hasn't happened to you. You might not have fired that employee, but tell me that your relationships with all your employees are exactly where they need to be. You can't do it, can you? I didn't think so.

None of us are perfect. None of us gets it right 100 percent of the time. We will certainly never get it right if we don't learn how to practice becoming effective in our communication patterns.

Yeah, Pat is a tragedy. It doesn't have to be that way and the good news is this: you can change it with a little effort.

The Power of Feedback

What's so funny is that many a person in my training programs will actually tell me, "My manager sucks. He doesn't set good expectations. He doesn't know how to help me perform. He doesn't provide feedback. He hurts me when he gives feedback because all he does is criticize."

Don't sit here and think that it's all on the employee to understand how to do the job; it's also on the supervisor who hired them. The supervisor needs to help them perform and do their jobs well.

That's what this book is about. It's about overcoming some of the challenges embedded within communication that are holding your organization back from performing. I remind you to really think about the examples that I've given you so far and the implications if you project them forward. If you do that with multiple employees throughout many years, what do you think happens to communication?

Always Develop Relationships

In the absence of relationship, feedback doesn't work. In the absence of relationship, communication is strained at best, ineffective at worst. Folks, we need to figure out how to do communication right. There's so much to this and we're going to cover it all! Stay with me as we explore the terrain of how to get into effective communication and do it right.

In a lot of my training courses, I teach people that you most need to develop relationships when you don't need them. The relational people in the room look at me like I've got three heads. I know they're thinking, *When would you possibly never need a relationship?* I look at them and say, "Well, you need to understand something. About 40 percent of the people in businesses are more task-oriented than they are relationship-oriented. They need to get results, not necessarily relationships."[7]

That's the reality of it. You've got to understand the importance of developing the relationships when you don't need them, which means develop them **now,** because you might need them later.

The concepts we'll explore in this book will not only help your communication skills; they'll help you be a whole, complete person who is effective in every dimension of your life.

Reflection

1. With whom do you find it difficult to communicate?

2. How have you damaged relationships as a result of a challenge in communication? How can you repair the damage?

3. Do you have any trust issues that need to be corrected? How will you approach these?

CHAPTER THREE

ARGUING FOR EFFECTIVE COMMUNICATION

When I train participants about communication, I ask them, "On a scale of 1 to 10, how good are you at communicating?" What often amazes me is that people will come back and say, "I'm a seven, I'm an eight, or I'm a nine." The challenge with those answers is in the next question. I ask them what communication is exactly, and they look at me like they've been caught with their hand in the cookie jar, because they haven't really considered what the question means. In fact, what they end up thinking is that communication is about speaking; how well they can convey a message to another human being.

The truth is that communication is a lot more sophisticated than that. There are many aspects to effectiveness in communication. In the diagram below, a mind map is presented that illustrates the dimensions of effective communication. The map contains all of the different things that you'll need to consider to really hone your skills. I want you to be a world-class master communicator; improving in these areas is how you get you there.

From the most fundamental level, people think communication is about talking. You can extend that from actual speaking to listening. If we go a little bit further, we can consider the fact that listening and speaking have a purpose, and the purpose is to create meaning and perhaps understanding. The way we do that is ask the other person questions while he or she is speaking: questions to clarify, questions to summarize, questions that help us understand. Meaning has to be transferred; understanding has to be created. When we think about communication, that's generally what we consider.

However, the process is actually much more complex. If you consider the average conversation with someone, it probably involves a series of clarifying questions for understanding. You might have to repeat yourself or offer a different example in order to explain a point. In addition, I think there has to be a process of feedback for communication to be effective. Further, there has to be something called **context,** there has to be a common ground that exists between the two parties.

Imagine this scenario: a chief financial officer (CFO) begins a conversation with a frontline employee. The CFO comes into the room and starts talking about balance sheets and return on investment and return on capital employed and the weighted average cost of capital and all these specific terms in the financial field. What is the operational employee going to understand? Yes, he understands that the language spoken is English, but he won't have context for any of the statements that were made. It might be that he never studied finance, so there is no shared context for this conversation.

At best, this conversation will be frustrating; at worst the CFO might make unfavorable assumptions (however unfairly) about the employee or incorrect actions might be taken, based on the interaction. I believe you have to walk a mile in someone else's shoes before you can understand what their message is all about. When you communicate, it is imperative that you have some level of understanding about your audience.

If you speak to an audience without considering them, I honestly believe it to be arrogant and, quite frankly, stupid. You need to understand your audience and communicate to them in a language they can understand. I'm not talking about dumbing your message down; I'm referring to the use of a common language, which will reduce complex terms into common sense. It's really important that you add the element of feedback and context to your model of communication.

Body Language

I read an excellent book titled, *What Every BODY Is Saying*. It's written by an ex-FBI negotiator, Joe Navarro.[8] In the book he outlines the different ways that FBI negotiators use to gain some insight into the state of mind of a suspect. One of the concepts that really stood out to me is the placement of the feet. The reality is when you're talking to another human being, if your feet are pointed toward the nearest door; chances are you don't want to be in that conversation.

If you're engaged in the conversation, your feet are pointed toward the other person. If you're uncomfortable with the conversation and want to exit stage right, so to speak, your feet will be pointed toward the quickest way out of there. This makes sense because, after all, your feet are part of your body and your body plays a major part of the communication process.

Often, people get a sense from your body language (whether you actually mean to communicate this with them or not) whether you're comfortable, whether you're uptight, whether you're nervous or anxious, or some other emotional state that says, "I don't want to be here right now," or, "I'm comfortable speaking to you."

Your body language is critically important to understanding your communication effectiveness. You could be saying all the right things with your words, but if you say it with the wrong body language, there's an old saying that goes, "Your body's speaking so loudly that I can't hear a word you're saying" (source unknown).

Emotional Intelligence

Another area about communication that I think is absolutely crucial has to do with the fact that communication is an interactive process. This allows you to modify the way you approach someone and modify the way you're communicating during the process. While you're communicating, you can consider context, change the way you're speaking, change the words you're using, speak slower, speak faster, change your vocabulary, alter your tone, or even switch languages. You can adjust the way you're communicating to make more impact, to get through to the person, and to create meaning and understanding in the conversation. In order to do this, there is a standard requirement. The standard is that you have to be aware in the moment. Awareness is such a critical component in the effectiveness of leadership or effectiveness of management within an organization.

The saying, "If you keep doing what you're doing, you're going to keep getting what you always got," is absolutely true. The beauty of growing your own self-awareness and your situational awareness is that you can recognize when somebody does not understand what you're saying and adjust your approach. You can recognize when someone is bored with what you're saying and adjust your approach. You can recognize when someone's getting angry about what you're saying and adjust your approach. If you adjust your approach, you stand a far better chance of not only being understood, but you also create a shared meaning with the other person, so he or she can take action based on what you're telling them. The concept of emotional intelligence was originally coined by researcher Daniel Goleman. He and two co-authors wrote an important book on the intersection of emotional intelligence and leadership called *Primal Leadership.*[9]

Emotional intelligence is one of the regulating factors that allows you to be effective when you communicate. Goleman defined **level one** of emotional intelligence as self-awareness. You have to be conscious of how you act, your emotional state, and your behaviors in the moment. Once you've achieved that state, he says **level two** of emotional intelligence is that of self-management. Think of those employees who like to push your buttons. You know who I'm talking about: they come up to you with the same old song and dance. Maybe they want to tattle on someone or tell you that what you need to have done "can't be done—it's impossible!" Whatever their story is, you've heard it before and it always sets you off. And here they come again! Self-management is about recognizing that this is the case and then choosing a different response.

Level three of emotional intelligence is becoming aware of your social environment. This has to do with fine-tuning your radar for the emotional temperature of your employees or your customers. I'm sure you're familiar with the expression, "read the room." This is what being socially aware means.

I recall a time when I was training a group of operational employees in a manufacturing firm. We were halfway through a training program and, honestly, I wasn't sure if they were buying into the material. In the midst of the class, one of the participants made an offhand remark about management not supporting them. I knew this was an opening to really connect with the class and help them get past a roadblock and actually grow.

I stopped the training class and asked what was really going on? The ensuing conversation started rough but soon the employees were venting their frustrations and eventually discussing how to move forward productively. My ability to read the room and see that there was something troubling the participants was critical to us moving forward successfully.

Level four of emotional intelligence is managing relationships and creating effective outcomes through those relationships. Are you perceived as likeable by most people, and are you able to work well with a diverse group? Well, then congratulations, you are probably already good at managing relationships. This level is all about developing others, managing conflict, and being an inspirational leader. Emotional intelligence is basically the ability to understand and manage your own emotions as well as those around you. You'll need to be strong in all these areas in order to be an effective communicator and leader.

Speaking of emotional intelligence, I want to address a related topic: your feelings. When you think about it, your emotional state can often play a dramatic role in the way you communicate. Strong emotions will shut your employees down, they will simply want to self-protect and get away from you. Maybe we should all take the advice of mothers around the world who say, "If you don't have something nice to say, don't say anything at all."

I know sometimes when you get angry, you just want to take on the world. Or maybe your motto is, "The best defense is a strong offense." Whatever your approach, you have to be aware of your feelings. Expressing your feelings, emotional intelligence, and body language are all interconnected. Once you develop and enhance these skills, you will be on your way to becoming a world-class master communicator.

Reflection

1. What is your definition of good communication?

2. Are you aware of your body language when communicating? What is your typical demeanor?

3. How would you assess your current level of emotional intelligence? Which area represents your most significant challenge?

4. What is your hot button?

CHAPTER FOUR

WHY WE FAIL

Where are several aspects of communication that are hidden: these are the facets of interaction that take place between your ears. I'm referring to perceptions, biases, assumptions, and filters—all of which can have a substantial impact on your ability to communicate.

Biases

A bias is obvious; you have a bias against somebody for some reason and often the reasons are subconscious. It is typically a prejudice you might have in favor of or against someone, a group, or thing. The connotation is usually considered to be unfair. A bias can cause you to look at the situation and create some meaning out of it without having all the information at your disposal. Unfortunately, these types of behaviors will lead to ineffectiveness in communication.

Biases are important to recognize and this has direct applicability to every level of management. It relates to the way people look at others from a leadership perspective. Often, we have what is known as an in-group and an out-group.[10] The in- group is those employees or those direct reports who you get along with; they're completely aligned with your perspective, your goals. They're easy to talk to; they're easy to delegate to. They get it done when you give it to them. They don't argue, they don't challenge, and they just get it done. If they do argue and challenge, it's usually for a valid reason and you typically appreciate it afterward. For the most part, this is your in-group, your go-to group that is often effortless to lead.

Unfortunately, you also have an out-group. The out-group is generally where you apply bias. You see, these are the people who are just difficult to communicate with. They're not aligned to the direction that you're trying to go; they might look, act, and speak differently than you; and they definitely think differently. All of these differences make it incredibly difficult for you to treat them the same way you treat your in-group. What inevitably happens is that you start to give all the plum projects and all the opportunities to your in-group, and you begin to view your out-group with an eye toward the need to punish and separate them.

In this case, it's bias that actually creates the problem. With a bias working against you, you might not see that the out-group represents diversity, and you might not provide them with the same opportunities to grow, learn, and perform at their highest levels. This type of bias is truly damaging and can have a lasting impact on an organization. As a manager, it is possible you have a bias against one group or another. The truth of the matter is, the more diverse your organization, the more powerful the ideas you can create and the more successful your organization can become.

American industrialist Henry Ford, the founder of Ford Motor Company, once said, "If both of us agree, one of us isn't necessary." If Henry Ford said that to you, who do you think would not be working at Ford the next day? I think that it's really important to embrace a diversity of opinion.

Doing so leads to the generation of new solutions and innovation within organizations. This hones and sharpens your strategies rather than just leading by groupthink stupidity because of the biases that you hold.

Filters

We always look at the world through the perspective of our own experiences. There's a simple example that I think will bring this to light. Imagine you're a young child and you're in a house with an old electric stove. You know what it's like when that burner or that element is on high; it creates a beautiful cherry red color. You know what happens when a child sees that beautiful color and can't resist reaching out to touch it—he burns his fingers. The reality is, because the child has little experience to draw from, he now associates the cherry red color with extremely hot things. He has created a filter based on his own experience.

Certainly, as we go through life, we recognize that some of those early filters are inaccurate, but they still exist. And the truth of the matter is, you might have a lot of them and they can cloud the way you look at people. Perhaps you look at an employee and think, *They're not good with numbers.*

I see people in training classes on a regular basis who say, "I'm not a good problem solver. I'm not a good artist. I'm not good at this. I'm not good at that." The simple fact is, ladies and gentlemen, there are filters that might be keeping you from your potential. There might be filters in communication, which ultimately keep you from effectively getting through to other human beings, because you're making assumptions about them and changing the way you communicate based on the filter.

No two human beings have the exact same experience, so our filters are different, which can lead to ineffective communication. I believe that when we make communication visual, we can eliminate some of the barriers that exist among people and can start to make understanding and meaning easier. As they say, a picture is worth a thousand words and a picture- based communication format can help people immediately understand what you're talking about.

Common Language

In many of my training classes, one of the things that I like to do is a communication exercise. It's a perfect example of the problems that are embedded in communication. It's a simple exercise. Take a 60- or 70-piece Lego car and split the group members into teams of two people. You'll have one person designated to build the car and the other person designated to give instructions. The two people are not facing each other. The person building the car cannot see the instructions, and the person giving the instructions cannot view the progress. There is no communication from the builder; she is not allowed to speak. The instruction giver is only able to give instructions, not answer questions.

I give the two people 10 minutes to build a car, and, inevitably, during the course of 10 minutes, it turns into an absolute train wreck. At the end of the exercise, we debrief and talk about the process and the problems each team encountered. We dig into the emotions and challenges that are present in the situation. The embedded challenges in this game are predictive of the problems in communication within an organization. Often there's no common language. What I found in this exercise is that there are three approaches that the **builders** take.

Give in: this is where the builders continue to put the pieces together, but they've really given in, they are just going through the motions, rather than trying to win the exercise.

Give up: they just quit altogether. They don't even look like they're trying to get it done. When they give up, they stay on the job and pretend to do their work, but they really don't giving you anything more than the minimum.

Give over: last but not least is fascinating, because they don't want to give in or give up. They realize that the game is rigged against them, so what they end up doing is they build whatever they want to build and have some fun. They continue to try to add value, but they don't do it in the context of the game, because the game is unwinnable.

This is a simple way that shows you the embedded challenges within communication. I show that when you can ask questions and you gain a common language, the builder can actually, in many cases, complete the car within 10 minutes.

If your employees understand what they're supposed to do and they have the opportunity to talk to you about what that is and how to do it, then the chances are greater that they'll give over rather than give in or give up. In the face of an apparently insurmountable challenge we want them to give over and keep trying to win! Communication is one of the first barriers to getting it done.

Now let's look at some of the other barriers that can get in the way of the effective transfer of information.

Pseudo-Listening Barriers

There are several barriers that are really important to understand. The first is called pseudo-listening. There's an excellent book on this topic, *Messages: The Communication Skills Book*, written by McKay, Davis, and Fanning.[11] I absolutely love this book, because it's a deep book on some of the practical skills of listening, including the concept of pseudo-listening. With pseudo-listening, you're not actually listening; you're just pretending to listen. There are many reasons why a person might pseudo-listen. Not all of these apply to a manager perhaps, but it's really important that you consider which one of these you might practice from time to time.

The **first** form is looking for specific information. Sometimes, when we're listening, we're really filtering out most of what's being said to us. We're only listening for specific bits of information. Maybe, we're just looking for the bottom line, waiting for the other shoe to drop, looking for that one piece of information that will allow us to make the next decision. Essentially, we're doing everything but listening to what is actually being said to us.

A **second** form of pseudo-listening is checking for signs of rejection. In negotiating contracts or dealing with an employee, we're looking for specific information or we're looking for a particular body language and the way they're speaking to us to see if whether or not they're accepting what we're telling them.

I had an employee apply for a promotion and when I interviewed him, he did not perform well during the interview. I remember the conversation afterward, where I had to break the news to him that he wasn't going to get the position. I decided to take a direct approach and said, "I just want to start by telling you that you did not get the position and I'd like to talk to you about what we can do together to prepare you for it the next time." What really struck me was his body language: you could literally see his eyes go down, go dark in the sense that he was tuning out, and he was no longer listening. He heard the specific information that he was waiting for and since it wasn't what he wanted to hear, he checked out. He was looking for specific information whereas I was checking for signs of rejection. As you can well imagine, the conversation did not go particularly well after that. I felt like I was talking to a brick wall.

A **third** form of pseudo-listening is based on the concept of wanting to be liked. This doesn't apply to every manager, but it's entirely possible that you are more of a social manager whose relationships play an important role in how they inform your decision-making process. During a conversation, in the back of your mind you might be wondering: does this person appreciate me or do they like me (especially if he's a tough one and you're sharing a difficult message).

A **fourth,** and perhaps the most common form of pseudo-listening and one that you will undoubtedly recognize, is preparing your response. This happens when someone else is talking to you and rather than listening, you begin to think about what you're going to say next and how you're going to respond. In my experience, this is one of the most fundamental forms of pseudo-listening. It's a potentially dangerous one, because you're preparing the response when you should be listening to what the employee is saying. As a result, you might speak to something he didn't say, because you're listening to the first part, but not the entire message.

A **fifth** form of pseudo-listening occurs when you listen because you want to be listened to, so you allow the other person to speak first. You might be listening in order to gather information or look for weaknesses in the other person's argument. Then when you hear what you want to hear (I've often heard this in conversations when someone says, "Aha, I knew you were going to say that!"), you pounce.

A **sixth** form of pseudo-listening is not knowing how to end a conversation. You might be familiar with this type, when you're dealing with someone who just doesn't know how to stop talking. You are done listening but you cannot find a polite way to bring the conversation to an end, so you keep pretending to listen while looking for an out.

All of these forms of pseudo-listening are the different ways in which we inevitably don't listen to another person. We're not actually hearing and listening with our whole body and understanding what someone else is saying. As a result, the other person in the conversation does not feel heard. In fact, it might give the other person a sense that we don't care or we don't understand.

It's important to be aware of these forms of pseudo- listening and we'll study them in depth in the next section of the book, when we delve more deeply into the importance of listening as a form of communication. In my opinion, listening is by far the most important aspect of effectiveness of communication.

Mental Models

Mental models are another form of barrier that relates to the filters that we create. As I've noted, we see the world through our own perspective.

Picture this: you see somebody in a retail establishment. They look to the right, look to the left, and then they place their hand in their pocket. What do you think just happened? When I ask most people this question, their response is usually to say, "Oh, they must be stealing something." What if the person was looking to the right, looking to the left, trying to find their spouse and they're putting their cell phone back in the pocket after ending a call? When I mention that possibility, the reaction is to say, "Oh, yeah, that's possible." Why is it then that we first assume they must be stealing based on the behavior that we see?

This is because of the mental models we have built for ourselves—we attribute what we think we would be doing in that circumstance and project it onto the situation. In most cases, the assumptions are generally not positive. It's really important that we learn to recognize the mental models that we operate from and check to see whether they are accurate or not.

Imagine an employee comes to your office and is clearly distracted. His shoulders are down, his head is slumped, and he is walking slowly. What do you think? *Oh, no, this is not going to be good; he is clearly upset about something. I bet he made a mistake, lost a customer, caused an accident, etc.* You start to add in information that is not there in order to understand what is going on.

Let's look at another example. Imagine you have an employee, Jane. Jane has just completed a significant project for you in support of a major strategic initiative. You receive her report, roll it into your summary of the initiative, and present it to your supervisor and the senior management team. You give credit to Jane in the meeting, praising her work and that of your team.

Later that day Jane is cool toward you and you cannot understand why. You have had a decent relationship with her up until this point. You ask her if everything is ok and she responds with a quick, "Fine!" and then excuses herself. What you don't know is that Jane overheard a conversation between two senior managers at the coffee machine. These two managers had heard your presentation and were impressed by the quality of the work you had done. Unfortunately, they were referring to the section that Jane had completed. She (un)reasonably assumed you had taken credit for her work and reacted accordingly.

Assumptions/Inaccuracy

A barrier that I really want to dig into is the one of assumptions and inaccuracy. There was a time when an employee came up to me (when I was a plant manager), and said, "You lied." My integrity warning alarm rang loudly in my head as I asked him, "Tell me more; what is it you think that I lied about?"

He said, "You told us that you would do the following and you didn't do it." I actually remembered the exact conversation he was referring to. What I had said was if the following situation occurs, *then* I would take a certain action. Unfortunately, he only heard, "I will do this." He didn't hear, "if the following occurs." As a result, because the precondition never materialized, I did not need to follow through on the actions.

This employee hadn't heard what I said; he only heard part of the story and made an assumption. When what he assumed would happen didn't happen, he chose to judge me for it. It's important to recognize that employees will often make assumptions and will operate from incomplete or inaccurate data. In doing so, they misunderstand what we say. It's so hard to communicate effectively, but that's the reality of being a manager in the business. You've got to overcome this problem and never operate under assumptions.

Imagine you're walking through your facility and you're five minutes late for your next meeting. As you go through the work area, one of your employees comes up to you and says, "Hey, I got this great idea! Why don't we do this?" You're in a rush, so you look at him and say, "You know what, that's a really good idea, I'll look into it," and you keep going. A couple of weeks later, you're walking back through that same area, and the employee comes up to you and says, "Hey, where are you on the idea that I gave you?"

You're looking at her thinking, *Huh?* You're searching your brain for a reminder, with a blank look on your face, while the employee realizes you forgot. Do you see the assumption embedded in the situation? The employee delegated a task to you, assuming that you, as the manager, would act on her idea. When you didn't deliver, as that employee assumed you would, she might begin to question your integrity, your commitment, and whether or not you'll get things done.

All of these barriers, assumptions, inaccuracies, and mental models that we operate from can cause problems in the way that we approach communication. As we move into the next section of the book, I'll give you some practical skills about how to become more effective in communicating. In the final section of the book, we're going to dig into some specific tools that you can practice and put to use that will get you outstanding results in your business.

Reflection

1. Where might you have a bias? How can you find out for sure? (Hint: feedback from a trusted peer.)

2. Which pseudo-listening approach do you practice? Don't worry; we all do them. The key is to become aware of it in the moment.

3. Are you unwittingly making promises you aren't keeping? Remember, these can simply be assumptions on your employee's part. What can you do differently?

4. How can you become more aware of your own blind spots?

CHAPTER FIVE

THE SNAFU PRINCIPLE

(Situation Normal All Fouled Up)

The fact that you have the ability to communicate does not equate to effectiveness in communication. To become effective you must learn and grow your communication ability.

There is an old quote "Two ears, one mouth, use them in that proportion" (source unknown). The quote reminds us about the power of listening, but I want to point out that just because we have a mouth and ears does not automatically make us effective communicators. However, as human beings, we all have the potential to communicate.

Communication is a skill, not a trait. It is not something that you're born good at. When you're a baby, one of the first things you learn to do is communicate your needs! As you grow and develop, your skills become more effective. You have to learn and practice in order to get better.

I was recently listening to a podcast interview of a communications expert, Julian Treasure,[12] who said the traditional Western education emphasizes the three R's—reading,(w)riting, and (a)rithmetic. Ironic isn't it that only one of those words actually starts with the letter R? Mr. Treasure observed that when you consider communication, two key elements were left out—speaking and listening.

Think about it, reading and writing are communication skills. In order to overcome the snafu principle you must recognize that you are not good at communicating unless you practice it and continually improve your game. Let's look at three real-life examples of how the snafu principle plays out.

Whiner Alert!

Did you know that complaining and whining are habits? It's a communication pattern. People express displeasure with their current situation. What they don't realize is that as they continue to practice this particular communication behavior, they're making the situation they're complaining about worse. I've never met anyone in business who actively looked forward to spending time and paying attention to somebody who complains and whines all the time. In fact, we tend to distance ourselves from this type of person.

I think every manager who's dealt with this type of employee realizes that eventually they're going to have to take some action. Wouldn't it be great if that employee—who is actually capable of doing his role—could be helped in some way to overcome the cycle of insanity, the snafu that he's living by communicating the same way every day, alienating people, and creating problems? What if he could turn it into a positive behavior and attract people who would collaborate with him and actually get results?

That's what we need. People who don't use the snafu principle and actually learn how to communicate effectively, recognizing that they are the problem.

Gen X Aspirations

I worked with an employee several years ago who was dissatisfied with his position—he wasn't a complainer or a whiner, per se, he just didn't like who he worked for or what he did. He had visions of grandeur; he thought, *I should be further along.* You know the type, right? A typical Gen X employee who had put in the time, did what he considered to be excellent work, and now he wanted to be rewarded. Rather than focusing on what he wanted, he focused on getting out of his current role.

He would apply for every position that became available in my company. **Every position**—it didn't matter what it was. Then he'd go through the interview process (if he got that far) and eventually be disappointed because the way he was communicating was ineffective. All he talked about was getting out of his current job instead of focusing on what he'd like to do next. He was ready to move onto the next big thing.

Unfortunately, if you have an employee who is trying to get out of something rather than trying to get into something (and they are different things), eventually the employee will get into a new position. But guess what? He's going to have the same fundamental problem, because you know what will come with him to that new role? He will. Eventually he will realize this position is no better because the chances are he doesn't have the right skill set to do the job. When he took the position, his focus was on getting out, not whether it was a good match for his skills. Eventually the cycle will begin again.

We ALL need to improve!

When you're practicing your communication, remind yourself that it's a journey, not a destination. The goal is communication excellence and effectiveness—which is something that you will continually strive to improve on.

I take a generally logical and sequential approach to communication. I see a beginning, a middle, and an end to the steps of a process. I remember one conversation where I was trying to delegate certain tasks to an individual. This particular person had more of a right-brain approach with random associations and a tendency to move the conversation all over the place, and then eventually circle back at some point to the original topic. Well, that is really frustrating to me. I get it and I understand there is a time and a place to be right-brained and creative and there's a time and a place to be left-brained and logical. The place that I was in, I needed left-brain logical and he wasn't giving it to me.

We kept going around in circles, with me continually saying, "Here is the series of responsibilities I need you to take on" and him nodding, but saying, "Hey! Have you ever considered . . ." and off he'd go on another tangent. In frustration, I began repeating myself. He finally looked at me and said, "Ron, why do you keep saying the same thing over and over?" Clearly I was frustrating him too! I stopped and I reflected (thankfully, he was silent). Eventually I realized, *Oh, my gosh, I know exactly why I've been repeating myself.*

I looked him in the eye and said, "Just as soon as I feel listened to, I'll stop repeating myself." He looked at me and said, "Oh, well here's exactly what you said: you want me to take on this responsibility and do this work within the business. That's what you want me to do, right?" I said, "Uh-huh. Yeah.

Will you do it?" He answered, "Yeah, absolutely." I said, "Okay. Then I don't need to repeat myself."

I was living the snafu principle by repeating myself. It took this moment, this defining moment to wake me up and realize why I was doing it and then not allow the frustration to overcome me and, instead, actually engage and solve the problem.

If you've got employees who continually repeat themselves, who say the same thing over and over and over; there's a significant possibility that they simply don't feel listened to. The next time you find yourself caught in a similar situation, try some active listening. Repeat back what you've heard so that the other person feels heard. Once you do, you'll find you've opened the door of communication and now you can actually talk to that person. If she starts to repeat a story, simply smile and say, "What else you got?" When an employee feels listened to, they will open up and listen to what you have to say.

The idea here is simple, yet it requires a lot of discipline and training to become an excellent communicator. Learn how to actively listen—to the point where the other person feels listened to—and then learn how to speak with clarity and conviction. The other person needs to be able to understand the passion that you have for a topic, so you must get to the point in a clear and precise manner such that the other person can understand.

As management consultant Peter Drucker said, "Communication is what the listener does." I don't care how eloquent you are. I don't care how well read you are. If you cannot get a message through to another human being, you simply have not communicated.

Communication is an intentional process. The whole point of the snafu principle is not to be reactionary and programmatic in the way that you communicate. The reason that most people just repeat themselves over and over and do the same thing and expect a different outcome is they're not consciously aware of their choices in how they're communicating. They're simply being habitual in their communication pattern and they're not thoughtful or intentional about creating a positive outcome in the first place.

Reflection

1. Where do you snafu? When do you find yourself being repetitive in communication?

2. Which of your employees might be suffering from a chronic lack of active listening? What steps can you take to change this outcome?

Part 2/Modeling Effectiveness

CHAPTER SIX

BASIC SENDER/RECEIVER MODEL

If you look at any text book on effectiveness in communication, you'll see a basic model that includes a figure of two people involved in a conversation. You have one person (called a sender) who has an idea they want to share and another person (called a receiver) who is the person that's going to receive the message.

The model is simple. You, as the sender, start with an idea that you want to share, but before you can actually share that idea you must first transform the idea (the thought of the idea itself), translate it, and encode it in such a way that it can actually be transmitted. The thought then turns into a sound wave through your voice, or perhaps it's an email through an electronic means, or a digital image. Whatever it is, you translate it into some format and then send it into the atmosphere through a process where it's going to be delivered to the other person.

The message itself is going to be transmitted through the environment and, unfortunately, there's noise in the environment. The noise comes in many different forms and that needs to be factored in to the process of communication. The message goes to the receiver and before she can understand the message, it first has to be decoded. The receiver takes the sound wave or image, translates it into her own brain waves and in so doing she now has the ability to understand the message that you sent.

The two people have completely different perspectives, they've got different backgrounds, they were raised differently, and they probably have different environmental factors that they've been exposed to. Despite the fact that they're working with a common language, they might not be able to understand each other at all.

This is one of the challenges we need to address when we start to look at effectiveness in communication. Shared experience is an important aspect of communication. It is sharing a language and context of a message. There's so much to really comprehend about how to make sure the other person understands.

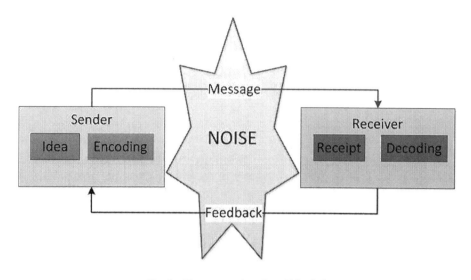

Basic Communication Model

(adapted from Cheryl Hamilton, *Communicating for Results: A Guide for Business and the Professions*)[13]

This model has a feedback loop that the receiver returns to the sender, where the message has to go back through that noise to the sender with the message, "Hey, I get it," or "No, I don't get it," or "Help me understand it better. I don't understand this piece," or maybe the receiver asks a question. The loop is not complete and the communication is not certain until the receiver has confirmed that she understands.

What's really fascinating about this process is that the sender can actually watch for signs of comprehension from the receiver. When someone is receiving a message, if he gives you the deer-in-the-headlights look it's fairly clear that he doesn't understand. Perhaps he has a furrowed brow or a quizzical look on his face that signals he's not getting it. Perhaps he's leaning in and putting his best ear toward the sender because there's too much noise in the environment and he can't physically hear the message.

There are many different ways, as a sender, that you can gauge whether or not you're being understood. You can look at the other person and begin to understand his body language and how he's demonstrating, through his actions whether he understands.

Management Speak

One of the things that managers often do in organizations is send messages in a particular way, where the message is sent through a language, a kind of a dialect of English. I like to call it management speak; it is a language only management understands. The average employee doesn't have an MBA degree. They don't talk about return on investment, cost of capital employed, internal rate of return, or all those fancy terms that managers must understand when they are at the top of their game. To the average employee, these words mean little to nothing.

Bottom line: employees just don't get management speak. Another of the challenges that managers have when they speak to employees is that their time horizon is different. The average manager is looking into the future. They're thinking about today, certainly, and getting the results they need to get today, but they're also concerned about next week, next month, next quarter, and next year. Really good managers are actually considering the next one to three years, not just the immediate future.

Now, if you think about your average employee, what are they interested in? What kind of questions do they ask you? I've asked this of many different organizations, literally to hundreds of managers: "What are the average questions that your employees ask?"

The three most common questions are:

1. Is there overtime? / May I leave early today?
2. What job will I be doing today?
3. Will you help me understand if my paycheck for this week is correct?

You see that their interest is focused on *now*. Their time horizon is on this hour, this day, and this week. On occasion, they might ask about their vacation allotment in the next quarter because they're thinking about vacation, but that is the exception. For the most part, an employee's primary interest is in the here and now.

Does that mean you can't talk to your employees about what's going to happen in the future? Absolutely not! I highly recommend it. One of the things that you need to focus on is starting your communication from the place where your employees can actually understand and connect with the message that's being shared. That means finding something that impacts them now and feature that early in the communication so the employees are engaged in the conversation.

That's one problem. Another challenge might be that your employees might not be educated in the same way. Their first language might not be English—for many, English is a second or even third language. There are those employees who are trying desperately to understand you. They have to translate into their first language and then translate their response back to you in English. Think about the delay that creates. It's important to recognize that there are many barriers to effectiveness in this particular part of the communication model.

Feedback can be another issue. How is it you ensure someone has understood what you say? A person (especially from a different culture) might acknowledge that she heard a message, but does that mean she understood the context and knows how to take the next step in the process?

You might be an eloquent and charismatic speaker, but if the people you're trying to communicate with have not understood your message in such a way that they can act on it, *you have not communicated*. It is that simple. That means the onus is on you—you need to be the one who creates a bridge of understanding, to make it so that the other person can understand.

From a manager point of view, it is absolutely critical that you understand and embrace this concept. Bottom line: if employees can't understand your instructions, they can't follow them. Who's ultimately responsible? You.

As a manager, you need to be able to communicate in such a way that your employees can follow your example and eventually excel through it. You are the sender in this model and it is your responsibility to ensure that the receiver has understood the message. In Chapter Eight, we'll look at speech patterns and how you can grab your audience's attention.

Reflection

1. How patient are you when communicating with those who speak differently from you?

2. How do you ensure meaning is transferred effectively when you communicate? What actions do you take? Are you consistent in this practice? How can you improve?

3. How do you respond to the deer-in-the-headlights look?

CHAPTER SEVEN

EFFECTIVE COMMUNICATION BEGINS WITH SELF-AWARENESS

Let's talk about the starting place of communication, because if you don't understand whether a person is grasping the message you're trying to send—if you can't recognize that up front—you will not be able to communicate effectively. Our journey toward effectiveness in communication begins with the concept of self-awareness. In that area it's really, really important that you understand how critical it is that your self- awareness be your guide to communication effectiveness.

Kevin Cashman, one of my favorite writers, wrote a book titled, *Leadership from the Inside Out.*[14] He tells the story of a priest walking through pre-revolutionary Russia. The priest, as he's taking his evening stroll, happens on a sentry. This sentry says, "Stop. Halt, who goes there?" All the usual stuff, except this sentry goes a step further. He asks, "Who are you? What's your purpose here? Where are you headed?" The priest, taken aback in the moment, thinks about it and a smile creeps across his face and he replies, "If I paid you, would you ask me those three questions every day?"

I think this is a really important story because the reality is we should always ask ourselves:

Who are you?

Where are you headed?

What's your purpose here?

The answers to these questions speak to the importance of having a high level of self-awareness: in every moment we have the ability to self-assess, self-regulate, and choose the best path. Many of us tend to go through life as robots just following a predetermined path of somebody else's design and not achieving much. How you grow self-awareness is really the key question that we want to dig into in this particular section.

In order to do so there's a model that comes out of neurolinguistic programming (NLP) that I'm quite fond of. The concept is called perceptual position and Robert Grinder first introduced me to it during a training workshop, in the early 2000s.

It's one of the starting places of neurolinguistic programming, which is a sophisticated study of human communication. I like to put it in practical terms as the study and mastery of holistic communication involving body language and mental positioning. The perceptual position model is really quite simple. It is looking at how we position our mind to interact with the world around us.

There are basically three positions.

1. Your mind can be focused on self-need or first position.

2. It can be focused on other need or when you're interacting with someone else, you're focused on that person.

3. Or, it can be in third position, observing the dynamics around you. Think of it like being a fly on a wall.

Let's walk through this model in a little more depth.

First position is when you're completely focused on self-need—it's all about you. You walk into a room and you're thinking about where you should sit. What's this going to be about? Am I going to be comfortable in here? Are the chairs comfortable? Is this going to be a fun engagement? Am I going to know anyone? The key in all of those statements is I, I, I. We're focused on ourselves. The reality of focusing on yourself is kind of unremarkable if you think about it. Most of us spend a good deal of time focused on self-need; it's just a fact of nature that we do.

However, as a manager of an organization, you need to be looking at the needs of your team members and focusing on what they're looking for. If you're stuck in first position, it leads to frustration on the other person's behalf. It leads to a lack of awareness, a lack of understanding of what's going on around you because you're just oblivious.

Think about the person who cut you off on the road. When you pull up beside them and you're a little frustrated, what are they doing? They're focused on themselves. Maybe they're talking on the phone or checking their email (hopefully not!); whatever they're doing, they're really not paying attention to what's going on around them. They're just focused on themselves.

It's actually a dangerous place for a manager to be. The risk here is that we're not aware of other people. That's really the problem and why I love to use this model in all of my in- person training classes to help people grow their self-awareness. You can't be aware when you're focused solely on yourself. That's first position.

Now, if we move into **second position** there's an old saying that fits this, "If you want to truly understand somebody, walk a mile in their shoes." That really is what second position is all about. It's understanding another person's perspective. You're tuned in to another person. When you do so, it gives you the ability to relate, to connect, to listen for and understand emotion. It allows you to really develop an effective professional trust-based relationship with them. The real advantage of second position is the boost it gives you in being able to build your own self- awareness of what's going on in the world around you.

The **third position** in this model, as I said earlier, is to think about a fly on the wall, an observer. This is not a detached observer, this is somebody who might be talking to someone and paying attention to the dynamics of what's going on around them.

Earlier, I wrote about the communication model and the self-aware communicator or manager. When she's talking to somebody and wants to check for understanding, she doesn't just look for a yes or no, I get it or I don't; instead she's paying attention to the eyes of the other person, the facial expression, the hands, and really trying to understand whether he gets it or not. Her position is about paying attention to the dynamics around her and it's not even necessarily just the person she's talking to. It's observing anyone else in the room, to see how they are behaving. It's really taking in the dynamics of what's going on around her.

Those are the three positions. Now what you can do with this is practice how to move from first to second, from second to third, from third to first, from second to third, and all the different combinations. One thing that you need to understand about this model is that it's not either/or. You can be in first position and also be in third position, speaking to someone else but paying attention to the dynamics and being the observer. You can partition your brain in such a way that this actually works. You can also be in second and third position, paying attention to the other person and also paying attention to the dynamics. The best listeners will be both in second and third positions at the same time. The best speakers will be in first and third positions at the same time.

An important distinction to recognize is that you cannot be in first and second at the same time. You're either focused on you or you're focused on them; you can't be focused on both. You can go back and forth really quickly perhaps, but you can't be in both places at once. This leads to a significant recognition: when we're listening, we need to shut up. We need to get out of first position and get out of all the pseudo-listening things that we talked about in the last section to really be present with the other person. You have to be actively listening and concentrating on what that person is saying when you're listening in such as way as to understand and demonstrate your understanding.

The power of this model lies in the choice of what our mental state is when we engage in communication. When you want to speak to an audience, you need to be able to access first and third positions consciously. When an audience asks you a question, you need to slip deliberately into second and third position, and then back to first and third position to answer the question. The ability to do this gives you a self-awareness that allows you to listen when you need to listen and speak when you need to speak.

Below is an exercise about perceptual positioning from my first book, *The First Questions: Coaching Your Way to Leadership Success.*

Perceptual Position Exercise

Objective: Through firsthand experience, learn to recognize and identify each of the three perceptual positions.

Materials: You will need some basic office products: sticky notes or nametag labels and colored pens or markers work well.

Setup: Each participant will need three stickers. Write number 1 in red on one sticker, write 2 in blue on the next, and write 3 in green on the third.

Separate participants into groups of three people. Identify two members to volunteer to be in first position for the first exercise. The remaining member will be in third position. Be sure participants place their sticker with the correct number on their shoulder so everyone knows what position they are in.

Have the two members in first position discuss something exciting that happened to them in the past week. The remaining member observes only. The two members in first person will, if correctly in first position, spend more time focused on what they want to say than on what the other person is attempting to tell them. Over-talking each other or going back and forth in one-upmanship manner is common here. Allow the conversation to continue for a few minutes.

Debrief

When debriefing the exercise, follow the questions.

1. What happened?
2. What emotions were experienced?
3. How did those emotions affect the approach to the exercise?
4. How effective were the interactions with the other participants?
5. What can be done differently in the future?

Reflection

1. How would you assess your self-awareness? How do you know this assessment is accurate?

2. What was your reaction to completing the self- awareness exercise?

3. In your own words, build a business case for the importance of self-awareness. Now pretend to convince your manager to build hers (don't actually do it ☺). Assess your business case. Was it strong? If not, redo it.

CHAPTER EIGHT

EFFECTIVE SPEECH PATTERNS

One-on-One

When you talk to individuals, it's kind of like a dance. During this dance, you want to be thinking about the conversation you're having. Is the conversation working? Are the two of you talking about the same concept? Are you actually in step with each other? Are you paying attention to the kind of visual clues that the other person is giving you? Are you in rhythm with the other person?

When you walk up to somebody to talk, how do you greet him or her? What opening lines do you use? Do you repetitiously use the same line every time or do you make it unique to each individual? Tailoring it to the individual is important. You need to be thinking before you get there about your intention, what points you are going to share, how you are going to get your message across, and (maybe most important), why this person should listen to you. I know you're thinking, *Because I'm the manager, I'm in charge, and they have to listen to me!* Recognize that while yes, you are the manager and they do have to listen to you, the deeper question relates to leadership. Think of it from the perspective of the person you are talking to: What's in it for them?

You want to ensure you have credibility with your employees. If you make promises that you don't live up to, it's entirely possible that they're going to tune you out when you start talking. It's a balancing act. You need to maintain the right level of credibility in order to maintain a professional, trust-based relationship with your employees, so they will want to listen to you. It's actually a really important key in the effectiveness of communication. Now, it does not mean they have to be your best friend. It just means that maintaining a trust-based, professional relationship ensures that your employees are likely to listen to what you have to say to them.

Structure of a Conversation

Are you going straight to the point? Are you going to tell a story or build an argument? What is your approach? It's really important that you consider this, because different approaches work with different types of individual. There are people who are more relational than others—they need to warm up in a conversation.

If you just go straight to an employee and say, "Hey, where are we on x?" it's entirely possible that in her mind, she's thinking, *Hi, how are you? Nice day we're having, isn't it?* When she does talk, she'll struggle to get to that point of the goal-oriented approach that you're used to taking.

And then, we have the technical individual. If you go to him and say, "Hey, how are you doing? How's your weekend?" his look gives away his thoughts, *Why are you asking me about my weekend? You should be talking about our business goal! We should be talking about the process.*

There is the outwardly expressive person who, if the greeting isn't enthusiastic and focused enough, might think there is a problem in the relationship. The key is to understand whom you are talking to and how to approach them individually.

How are you going to close the conversation? One of my favorite acronyms for how to close any conversation or meeting or presentation, is called WDWBW: Who does what by when? I think it's really important to have that in your back pocket, because what it does is allows you to make sure that you know who's got action items walking out of the meeting. Another acronym that I like is CICOYS: Can I count on your support? I think it's important to make sure that your employees stand behind you in support.

It is difficult enough talking to one person, so what about groups? Well, a group is made up of individuals, and those members might have different needs. You'll want to assess those needs and possibly adapt the message to meet any individual requirements, if possible. I also want you to pay particular attention to body language, both yours and theirs.

Body language is a good clue as to whether they're actually getting what you're saying and listening to your message. In this next section we'll cover how to get a group's attention (the good kind), how to create an introduction and a core message that are designed for effectiveness, and, finally, how to conclude with a summary and call to action.

Attention!

First, how do you get the attention of the group? Second, how do you introduce the topic? Third, how do you keep their attention? Fourth, what happens if you lose your audience's attention?

How do you get the attention of the group? What you're going to find is a majority of your employees are focused on their own needs; they're focused on themselves. They're not focused on you when you first arrive in the room. Especially when you're talking to front-line workers. If you just start talking without some form of introduction or getting the audience's attention, you're likely to find that your group isn't listening to you, at least not the majority. There are a variety of ways to do this, including the following:

Start with a greeting: Say, "Hello, how are you doing?" One of my favorite ways to greet a group in my training classes is to shake everybody's hand before I start the class. What this does is create a connection between me and the people in the room. I also like to introduce myself: "Good morning, everyone, I'm Ron Hurst. I'm going to be your speaker today," or " Hey, everyone, I'm Ron, we are going to have a meeting on x." As a manager, you probably don't need to introduce yourself to your employees—they should know you. If they don't, you've got some work to do, and I recommend you go back to my first book, *The First Questions*.

Lower your voice: I encourage you to lower your voice the next time you are in a big group. I believe that the more we have to raise our voice over the noise to get heard, the less you earn your employees respect. So, if you find yourself thinking, *I'm going to yell to get their attention,* I think you've got some work to do in the respect and credibility area.

Make eye contact with silence: Another way that I quite like is to ask for everyone's attention and then make eye contact with somebody in the audience who's actually paying attention. Just smile, and stand in the silence. What will happen inevitably is that person who you're smiling at will start to shush everybody and ask others to pay attention. "Hey, shhh, he's getting ready to start."

Command attention: You could yell at them. "All right, quiet down, we're going to start. Hey, shut up in the back!" But, I'm going to caution you, anytime you have to forcefully gain control of a group, you're eroding your own credibility by subtly (or not so subtly) disrespecting the individuals and the group. So, be really careful.

Whichever attention-grabbing device you use, always use polite and respectful ways of getting the group's attention. And be patient as you do it. As you start to gain their attention, if you can consistently apply some of these techniques, you'll find that they will slowly change their behavior toward how they come into the room with you.

I like to introduce the topic with one sentence or one central message. I want to tell them what it is, "All right, we're going to be talking about this today. We're going to have to make this decision and this decision. And this decision that is ultimately about this topic." This gives everyone a reason to pay attention and to know what you're going to be talking about.

Speaking of attention, have you thought about why this group needs to pay attention to what you say? I get it, you're the manager—but again, you're looking for the hook that makes them want to pay attention. As a manager, you generally already have credibility by the position you hold. If you have lost it, however, because you made promises you didn't keep, or for whatever reason you don't have the credibility of the group—you need to think about how to build it. It's important that you have the credibility in order to be able to speak to a group of employees.

Let's look at how to plan the way to speak to a group. There are many excellent resources on this topic. I must give credit to the University of Pittsburgh website and to author Cheryl Hamilton, both of whom influenced my thinking in this area.[15]

PPAWS

I have an acronym that I love to use called PPAWS. The first P stands for **purpose**, the second P stands for **presence**, the A for **audience**, the W for **win-win**, and the S for **structure**. I think that if you begin to consider these five letters, and what they mean, you will get much better at communicating.

So, for instance, you need to establish a clear **purpose** for your message. I've found that writing down the message helps to clear the points in my mind. I know that if I struggle with putting it down on paper, I'm going to struggle with sending a clear message to the group. By writing, it clarifies the purpose in your own mind and it will make it easier for you to convey.

I also want you to think about a military acronym—BLUF: Bottom Line Up Front. This is a powerful way to communicate. Especially when you are speaking to peers or your manager. As you know, we have a limited amount of time as managers and it's important that we get to the point quickly. So, share the bottom line up front: give them the bottom line and then explain the background of it.

Next is **presence**. You want to make sure that you're confident in your approach. Does your body language match the confidence in the message you're sharing? Use a clear tone, vary the pitch of your voice, and vary the volume that you use to amplify certain points.

Also, it's wise to speak slightly slower than you normally do. What you'll find, depending on how comfortable you are speaking in front of a group, is that your nerves might get the better of you. When you're nervous, you tend to speak a little bit faster. So, speaking slightly slower than normal, thinking about speaking slower than normal, will bring it back down to a normal conversational pace.

Be careful about the filler and nervous tic words, the um's and the ah's. Some people use the word "like" or "right," and these are all just a habit that we get into, but they're distracting to the message that you're sharing. Be careful with those.

Make sure you're standing and making clear eye contact with everyone in the room. Obviously, not all at once. But you want to just make eye contact with everyone throughout the message. When it comes to eye contact, I've discovered there are four different approaches.

1. The **first** is not to make eye contact at all. Some knucklehead has offered the wisdom to set your eyes just above the heads at the back of the room. I'm telling you, the people in the room can tell that you're not looking at them, so don't do that.

2. The **second** is to make eye contact with only one person, usually a power person. This is not a good idea.

3. The **third** way to make eye contact is to look at only half the people in the room and ignore everyone else. It might seem like the speaker is looking at everyone, but she's not. This approach is not good.

4. The **fourth** way is to scan the room looking at individuals, which is the appropriate way to make eye contact.

I also want you to make sure that you use the space in front of you purposely, not nervously. There were times when people did presentations in my classes and it's like they were dancing. I mean it's really quite distracting. It's just a nervous pattern of walking back and forth, back and forth. If there is someone in the audience who has a specific interest in a point you plan to make, walk over to them and look at them as you're making that point, and then come back into the power position. This is a subtle yet powerful way to emphasize a key point. Walk to the slide projector, the screen if you're using PowerPoint, and point at a certain bullet point from time to time. Use the space purposely.

Next is your **audience**. Who is your audience? What is their level of understanding in the context of the message you're about to share? This is really important. Many people overlook this point. You need to realize that your employees don't have the same access to knowledge that you do. And sometimes, you talk from your experience and your knowledge and don't think about the fact that your audience might not have the same experience to draw on.

Earlier in my career, I got called into my general manager's office. I had only met the man twice. Once he tore a strip off me over something minor, and the second time he hired me into the position I was in at the time. So, I didn't know how to take it. I mean it was fifty-fifty as to how the meeting would go!

I walked into his office, he looked at me and said, "Ron, sit down." I sat down. And then he looked at me and said, "I just want to let you know, you weren't affected." Now, I'm sure all of you can imagine the question forming in the back of my head, and I wanted to scream, "By what?"

I looked at him and I calmly said, "By what, Bill?" He looked back at me and said, "Oh, yeah, that's right, you don't know. Our organization's going through a lay-off, and I wanted to let you know, you weren't affected. But one of your employees is, and I wanted to talk to you about that."

You see, managers often have access to information that the audience (employees) of the message doesn't have. You need to think about what their understanding of the context is. If you just go off talking about something, unless they all have the same level of knowledge you have, you will quickly lose them.

Now that you've considered the context of your message, it's time to consider your audience's likely attitude toward the message that's being shared. Is it a positive or negative message? If it's negative, it changes the way you want to present it. It changes your preparation. If you have people in the audience who are going to fight you about the message that's being shared, you want to make sure you anticipate their questions and prepare for them. It's really important.

Next, you need to establish who in the audience is an influencer. Who's going to be the person an audience member goes to for clarification about the message? As a manager, I often made it a point to know who the influencers were and I would talk to them a couple of minutes before the meeting to let them know what was going on. Just so they could share it from the perspective that I was sharing it from.

Some other aspects you want to consider in terms of your audience include the following:

- What is the age of the audience? Is there a wide range?
- What is the audience gender?
- What is the educational level? The ethnicity? The political stance?
- Are the audience members stressed?
- What are they interested in?
- What's their likely attitude?
- What time of day is it? You think the time of day doesn't matter, but, if you have a meeting at 11:45 and you expect to hold people's attention, when all they can think about is where they're going for lunch, you're going to struggle to maintain their attention.
- If they're sitting in a room, are the seats comfortable?
- Are they hungry?
- What's the likely mood?

All these things matter whether the people can actually listen and accept the message that is being shared.

The next step is to look at the message from a **win-win** perspective. What's the win for the audience? What's the win in the communication with the audience? In order to find this, we have to look at the communication from the listener's point of view. And everybody's favorite radio station, WIFM or What's in it for me? plays a role. If you can look at the message from the point of view of the audience, and feature the benefit to the listeners somewhere early in your message, your audience will pay more attention.

This is one of the most powerful ways of drawing somebody out of the first position. To draw them out, you need to give them a reason, something of personal benefit for them to listen to you. Here's a really interesting perspective: what if you can't find a win for the audience? How do you think the people are going to react to the message that you're about to share? I guarantee you they're not going to be all that positive about it. So, it's something to think about as you prepare to share your message.

Finally, we want to think about the **structure**. I already mentioned the bottom line up front (BLUF) approach. There's a related approach called bottom line explanation and impact. You could structure your message with a beginning, a middle, and an end. You might provide a bullet-point list. You can tell a story or a parable. It's really a powerful way of making a single point or stressing a cultural element point. You might use the newspaper approach. Tell them what you're going to tell them, then tell them, and then tell them what you told them.

How will you approach the structure? It is important to be intentional about having structure. Simply opening your mouth and hoping for the best is a really bad idea when it comes to communicating effectively. This is how snafu communicators approach it.

The Critical Point

So, how do you conclude your message? How do you summarize? This is one of the most critical aspects. I don't care what the message is; it's critical that you close well. If you were to do a little survey and ask people to memorize ten random numbers, they would almost certainly remember the first number, and they will likely remember the last number. Anything in the middle is a crapshoot. They are not going to remember, unless they have an eidetic memory or something of that nature. What that means is the last thing you say, had better not be: Are there any questions? The best way to end is to sum up, highlight the most important point.

You want to end the message with a call to action. You'll start with a signpost. A signpost tells people, "All right, if you've not been paying attention to this point, pay attention now." A call to action states, "All right, here is what I need you to do as a result of this meeting." You reemphasize the key point. Always end the message with the most important aspect—the key point you want to leave them with.

Airplane Service: There are several things that we need to consider when communicating with people. As you know, a good airplane flight has in-flight service. And when I talk about in-flight service on a flight, this is a metaphor for how you share your main points of your message. The things I would like you to be thinking about when you're talking to a group include the following: Don't bore them—if you're one of those engineer kind of managers, analytical in nature, I want you to be really conscious of your tone of voice. And be aware of the way that you inflect your voice, when you bring it up and you bring it down. I want you to move it around so it's not so monotonous and consistent that people start to fall asleep when you talk.

I also want you to be conscious of the fact that when you're standing in front of a group, especially if you're giving a presentation with PowerPoint, do not read the slide and don't read note cards. You should know your message well enough that you can speak with ease and clarity without a secondary reference.

You definitely need to maintain great eye contact. And one of the things about eye contact that's really important to recognize is to determine what the right amount is. In my training classes, I often talk about it being somewhere between a restraining order and none at all. The reality of how much eye contact you make is that you should reciprocate with the amount of eye contact that your audience is making with you. If it's more than that, you'll creep them out. Less than that, they'll start to wonder about your confidence.

In-Flight Service: If you need something on a flight, you want the attendant to come and give it to you right now—not ten minutes from now. Remember to smile and when someone asks a question, answer it when it's asked. That's an important little point. It might mess you up a bit, if you're talking about a subject that's going to take a while to get through. But I want you to recognize, it's important to answer the question as it comes up. This will allow you to maintain a sense of conversation with the audience rather than some formal stiff approach.

Aborted Takeoffs: I want you to avoid the aborted takeoff. Make sure you practice for a smooth takeoff so that you have your audience's attention. The worst thing you can do is start talking, then go back and say, "Hey, wait a minute, I've started already. May I have your attention?" That is an indication that you might not have their attention or their respect.

Turbulence: I also want you to avoid turbulence. Don't lose your place. If you do get lost, take a deep breath. And what you'll find is that taking a deep breath will get you out of that anxiety mode and you'll be able to get back to where you lost your point. Avoid the red eye. Definitely avoid putting your audience to sleep by providing way too much detail. Manage your timeline and speak with enthusiasm. Be done, when you say you're going to be done.

Diverted Flights and Weather: As you know, airplanes sometimes have to divert to an alternate location. Be really careful about this. This is related to unnecessary tangents. Don't go off on too many tangents that lose the attention of your audience. Remember, you've got a destination in mind, and you've got to get there. Another airplane flight to avoid is the one that goes through bad weather. If you're working with other managers in your presentation, you want to make sure it's smooth and not turbulent so that you transition from one to the next smoothly and efficiently.

Holding Patterns: You want to avoid being stuck in a holding pattern, circling the airport, not knowing how to close. This is actually one of the most dangerous things you can do. Be sure to plan for a smooth landing. Know how you're going to close and keep to the script. Above all, don't make a bunch of promises you can't deliver—if you find yourself nervously chatting away, take a deep breath and end the message promptly.

Reflection

1. Be honest, how much of the concepts presented above do you *intentionally* practice in day-to-day communication? How can you improve your consistency?

2. What are some of the ways that your conversations are flights no one would want to take? What steps can you take to practice improving in this area?

CHAPTER NINE

EFFECTIVE LISTENING

Self-awareness gives us a remarkable opportunity. When we're listening to others, it gives us the opportunity to know how they're behaving and how they're feeling because we're more in tune with where they're at and, as a result, we can become an even more effective listener. Likewise, when we're speaking we can also assess the degree to which others are listening to us and tracking the story, and if we have a high level of self-awareness, we can adjust the way that we communicate to make sure that meaning is transferred and that they understand the message that's being conveyed.

That's one of the main reasons why I believe that awareness is such an important part of communication. In this chapter I want to dig into the importance of listening. I think all of us have experienced, at one time or another, the feeling of talking and feeling like no one was actually listening.

Is anyone really listening?

There's a training exercise I do when I teach people how to listen. I split the group into twos and designate one as the listener and one as the speaker. The speaker is handed a script and I pull the listener aside to give instruction (which includes telling them to do everything in their power to be the opposite of an effective listener! I encourage them to check their phone, not make eye contact, and be completely distracted).

The first time I saw this exercise play out, it was between two managers. The manager who was the speaker became so utterly frustrated with the manager who was listening that he threw a pen at him while screaming, "PAY ATTENTION TO ME!"

This story is so appropriate for our fast-paced world where information's coming at us at a ridiculous rate and we have to make choices about what we listen to and what we let into our brain. What suffers are the relationships with those people who—if we just listened to them—we would develop deeper bonds and help them perform at their highest level.

I think everyone suffers from a lack of being listened to and, as a result, there's this constant low-level frustration, so that when an opportunity to be listened to arrives and it doesn't happen, they get disappointed again and shut down. As a manager you need to understand that this is more than just touchy-feely stuff. This is actually hard management skill. This is the ability to listen to an employee to help him or her feel valued enough to want to give you more discretionary effort than the minimum.

Now if I had a buck for all the managers who told me that they wanted to know how to motivate their employees, I would be a rich man. My answer is consistent and simple.

- Treat them like human beings, and treat them with respect and dignity.

- Help them to perform at their highest level by respecting and valuing who they are.

- Recognize that they are no different than you are, other than they have a different level of responsibility and perhaps a different skill level.

Listening is the cheapest form of motivation and the most powerful. How does real listening compare to what most of us do (which is pseudo-listening)? They look like the same thing to the uninitiated. To somebody who doesn't know what listening is, they won't be able to tell the difference. They'll feel it, but they won't know why they're feeling frustrated or detached or disconnected from the other person.

Pseudo-listening lacks the real connectivity that you get when somebody actually tunes in and listens to what you have to say; tracking your story. Real listening involves your whole body. It is not just your ears. I think this is the greatest differentiation between hearing and listening. Hearing involves your ears. Listening involves your entire body. It is active and it is hard work. In the end, it is a true gift to another person.

During the training programs I teach, inevitably at least once per class, one or two of the participants will share with me that what they're learning helps them in all aspects of lives. You see, while this book is about how to manage effectively, I want you to recognize that people are whole beings and the old mindset that encouraged you to check your emotions at the door is another example of my favorite technical term. It's stupid.

You're a whole person. Anyone you deal with is a whole person. If you deal with whole people instead of pretending that parts of them don't exist, you'll have a far better chance of motivating them to perform at a high level. Real listening is hard work. Pseudo-listening is not where we want to be and, unfortunately, this is where most of us are when we're listening at work. We sense that there are far too many things to do and not enough time to do them, so we multitask while we listen. The end result is we're only giving partial attention.

Why We Don't Listen

The questions I have for you are: "Who do you have the most difficulty listening to? What are some of the typical reasons that you have difficulty listening to them?" It might be that you're listening simply because you want to be liked: you want to feel like you belong. You might listen because you're checking for signs of rejection from the other person. The relationship matters to you at a level where you're checking for signs or rejection. These two might not have a lot to do with management, but they certainly do in regular everyday relationships between peers, between you and your supervisor, and also outside the workplace.

You might be pseudo-listening because you're just looking for specific information. For example, when you're conducting an investigation for human resources (HR), you're looking for specific information, trying to figure out the real cause. Who was the instigator? What actually went down? In fact, in that case you might even be looking for specific clues that lead you to be able to find holes in the story, which is another one that we'll also talk about.

One of the most common reasons that people pseudo-listen is that they are preparing their response. They stop listening partway through and begin thinking, *How am I going to counter; how am I going to respond; what am I going to say to that?* They effectively stop listening and start thinking about how to respond and only give partial attention.

There are other people who listen to be listened to, so it's a quid pro quo arrangement where if I listen to you, then you should listen to me. Again, it's similar to wanting to be liked, but not something that I would expect from a decent manager.

We might be listening as a means of gathering ammunition, looking for weaknesses in an argument or trying to figure out what someone is saying that might contradict a story. Lawyers are good at this, but as managers, we get good at this one too.

Think about if you're negotiating a claim or working on negotiating a contract with a supplier. You're looking for weaknesses in the sense of trying to create a stronger bargaining position. You might listen only to understand your impact on the other person, and I guarantee you that there are many managers, self-aware managers, who do this.

You need to understand your impact on the other person simply because you don't know if you're being understood. So you might be listening to the other person just to see what impact you've had on that person and whether your message is getting through.

Alternatively, you might be listening to someone out of politeness: you want to be nice rather than abrupt. Some people have what I call a pendulum perspective. They think if they're not being nice, then they're being rude. As a manager, you deal in shades of gray. It's rare that there's a yes or no answer, one extreme or the other.

The last reason you might be listening is because you simply don't know how to end a conversation. You want to be polite and professional, yet the other person will not stop talking.

At this point I want you to take a moment to evaluate yourself on how you handle conversations with those you speak with on a regular basis. As a manager, I suggest that you look at your general manager, your supervisor, a peer, and a direct report, and maybe a supervisor or an individual contributor who you struggle to listen to. These titles might differ in your organization.

Let's walk though these groups with an example from each of them and answer honestly which of the types of pseudo-listening you struggle with to see if there's any pattern.

Do any of these pseudo-listening techniques come up repeatedly for you or does it vary with different people? Your response will give you some insight into the work that's needed to become an effective listener.

Five Points of Listening

There is a basic model of listening that I like to follow when I teach the listening concept. This model is an adaptation of the excellent model presented in the Mind Tools™ website.[16]

Listening involves five interrelated points. It's not a step- by-step model. There are just five things that we need to be paying attention to.

The first is **pay attention**. This might seem obvious, but it amazes me how many people screw it up.

The second point is that we need to manage our **body language**. We need to be conscious of the fact that our body speaks as much as our voice does when it comes to listening.

Feelings and content is the third point. What I have found is that some people are really good at listening for content and then there are others who are really good at listening for feelings, these are the people who are more empathetic in nature. It doesn't matter which one you're better at. The reality of listening is we need to get good at both.

The last two steps go together, **provide feedback** and **respond appropriately**. These are more about how we demonstrate that we have listened in a verbal and visual sense. We're going to dig into each of these five points in a little more depth.

Pay Attention

You need to pay attention to the speaker. You need to give your undivided attention. What does that mean exactly? Well, you know that cute little cell phone that you have in your hand, the thing that you bring to every meeting, that you text people on and check for important email? If you are going to listen to someone and mean it, I highly advise you turn your cell phone on silent, on vibrate, and put it in your pocket or put it in your desk and don't look at it. I think that we can all do with some technology downtime for at least 15 minutes once in a while to actually listen to someone.

Now, you might not agree with me on this point, but I guarantee you the minute you answer the phone in the presence of an employee who's got something important they want to say, you're saying to them: there's somebody more important that I need to be in conversation with right now other than you. Is that really the message that you want to send to your employee? Employees who believe that they are important, who believe that you care about them, who believe that they're respected and provide value to the company: guess what they want to give you more of? Their discretionary effort.

You definitely want to give them your undivided attention free of technology, whether it's a laptop, a traditional computer on a desk, a phone, a pager, whatever it is, just don't be distracted. Give them your undivided attention. Acknowledge the message by actually letting them know that you're hearing what they're saying. It might be about nodding. It might be about repeating back what you've heard, but it's recognizing the other person speaking and letting them know that you do actually hear them and you are listening to them.

An important aspect of paying attention is managing the various patterns of pseudo-listening that we all fall into at one time or another. How do we do that? All the different forms of pseudo-listening that we've talked about are mental, meaning that they're all decision or choices that we have made.

If you've made a choice to prepare your response, if you've made a choice to filter for certain information, if you've made a choice to look for holes in their argument, etc., then you can similarly make a choice to *not* do that and actually listen to the person instead. It's a mental exercise. It requires discipline and the ability to make a choice in the moment. I go through a little routine when I want to pay attention during an important conversation.

- I turn my computer screen off.
- I turn off my phone and put it in a drawer.
- If it's an important personal conversation, I might even remove my watch. (Though I don't recommend doing that at work!)

Removing the environmental distractions makes it far, far easier to pay attention and focus on the employee.

Body Language

Point number two is focused on demonstrating that you are listening through your body language. What do I mean by this? It might mean nodding, it might mean making appropriate facial expression. Now, I'm not the most empathetic person in the world, so sometimes it's good to have a clue if someone's telling a sad story, maybe I'll put a bit of sad face on. If they're excited, maybe I want to have a look of excitement or a smile and some pleasure. Whatever it is, just make appropriate facial expressions that track the story.

You also want to maintain an open posture toward the other person. When you get closed off by crossing your arms and leaning back in the chair, it sends a message that you're not listening anymore, so you really need to manage your body language in order to help the other person get the message.

If you're sitting, I highly recommend sitting facing your speaker, and I've often heard it called a seven-degree lean. It really gives the nonverbal sign that you're leaning in to listen to something important. You don't want to lean away or get creepy and lean too far forward. You just want to lean in enough to show interest. The one separation I'd like to make on this point is that if you're standing with an employee, you also can do this face-to-face, looking straight at them, but I've also seen it done well where you can walk side-by-side and have a meaningful conversation too. I think when you're standing, there's a little more leeway, as long as your focus is on the same point that the person is focused on. If you're both walking toward something in the distance, you're both focused toward that. You're not looking off to the side or looking down at the ground or the ceiling, whatever it is.

If you are facing a person, obviously you want to make eye contact. Eye contact is such an important point of listening. Now, in the North American cultures, especially in Canada and the United States where my career has been spent, I have noticed that when people don't make eye contact with us, we tend to judge them.

In my training classes, I always ask: "If somebody doesn't make eye contact when they walk up to you, what does that say to you?" The quick responses are that the person can't be trusted. They lack integrity. They're hiding something.

It's said that the eyes are the windows to the soul and I think subconsciously if we don't make eye contact with someone, it's usually because we do have something, some reason why we don't want to make eye contact. Keep in mind the importance of eye contact when working within an American or Canadian business. People expect it and not doing it has a negative connotation that you don't want to give. It also goes with listening.

Another question I ask during my training classes is: "How much eye contact do you make?" Most people say they make plenty of eye contact, but, really, no one knows the exact right amount.

There's a case study in one of the classes that I teach about organizational behavior that addresses this question. In the case study, female clerks at a grocery store filed a suit against their employer because the employer required them to both smile and make eye contact with all guests.[17] Actually, I believe they said that they had to do so for at least three seconds. The reality was that with the female customers, this was not a big deal. It's just a friendly standard.

Unfortunately, many of these female clerks, after smiling at male customers for at least three seconds, felt that they were then being harassed by the customer. Because of the store policy, the clerks were being followed through the store by customers and asked for their phone numbers. So, the right amount of eye contact just depends.

I tell people in my training classes that it's somewhere between a restraining order and none at all. The right answer is approximately the amount that the other person is making with you. As a manager, you'll find that you can make a little more eye contact with the employee, and it really sends a powerful message about the confidence that you have in your position and the relationship you have with that person. So eye contact is a subtle, but important, point of body language in effective listening.

Feelings and Content

You want to listen to both the content and the feeling of the message. I talked about this earlier, that we want to listen to the content of the message so we can understand what the employee is actually saying. But have you ever noticed that sometimes an employee will come to your office and complain about one thing and you just know in your gut, that's not the reason why she's there?

You really need to listen to the content of the message, but you also have to listen to the feeling behind the message. What is it she is really trying to say? You need to acknowledge the emotion that you think you're hearing. You can do this in a harmless way by saying, "Wow, that customer complaint, you must be really frustrated." Or, "Wow, you lost three hours of production time and it cost you your monthly bonus? You must be upset or disappointed in your performance."

Just acknowledge the emotion you're hearing in her voice. There is a really useful resource for this that you'll find in a great workbook I referenced previously called *The Messages Workbook: Powerful Strategies for Effective Communication at Work and Home* (see note 16). The authors offer a model of characterizing emotions we experience into four groups: glad emotions, mad emotions, sad emotions, and bad emotions. When we acknowledge the emotions that the people are feeling, somehow this gives them permission to breathe, gives them permission to continue, and that they are being understood.

Now, an important distinction to make here is that just because you're acknowledging the emotion doesn't mean you have to agree with it. It doesn't mean that you're saying they're right. Acknowledging those emotions gives them the opportunity to get through the message rather than being stuck with this emotional dam in their head or in their heart. Also when you're listening, you've got to manage your own emotions. Don't get defensive and fall back into pseudo-listening mode. It's essential that you manage your listening patterns if someone is sharing their feelings with you.

Provide Feedback

This point is about demonstrating that you've heard what was said and you understand it. This might take the form of asking specific questions or you might summarize the points from time to time. Honestly, one of the things I've found that works when you're speaking to someone who suffers from verbal diarrhea is to simply say, "I know you've got a lot to share with me, and I want to hear it. Could you please summarize the most important points in twenty-five words or less?" I guarantee that if you practice that on a consistent basis, you'll actually help that employee to dial in their communication. This is another explanation of the snafu principle, as many people have not actually taken the time to think about how they communicate. And because they haven't thought about it, they just talk out whatever thoughts pop into their heads.

They haven't thought through how to structure the message. They haven't thought through how to compose it in such a way that it maximizes the chances of it being understood. They just open their mouths and hope for the best. If you help them with the discipline of actually starting to think it through and summarizing the message, you'll be doing them a favor by getting them to actually think about the way they communicate and start to get better at it.

Another important aspect of providing feedback comes in the form of encouraging remarks. You want to encourage others during a conversation by saying, "Oh, really?" or "Then what happened?" This feedback let's a person know that you're tracking the story and encouraging them to continue sharing.

Respond Appropriately

The fifth and final point in the effective listening model is to respond appropriately. First, be respectful and honest. Let me go off on a tangent for a moment. I've met managers in the past who have used a line that really astounds me. They'll say, "Well, don't ask me for my opinion if you're not prepared to hear it." While this might sound like tough talk and straight candor, I actually think it's a bully tactic and completely inappropriate for the workplace.

Just because a person is asking you for feedback doesn't give you the right to be rude, disrespectful, or hurtful. I don't see how that helps a business at all. Now, is it possible to convey a difficult message to someone and still be respectful? Can you criticize and be respectful? The simple answer is absolutely.

I recall a story about when I had to discipline front-line employees as a manufacturing operations manager. I'm sure all of you do this on a regular basis. One of the things that I would always do is I would make sure the discipline I was giving was fair and deserved. If there was doubt, I tended to pay more attention to that employee, shall we say, rather than be quick to crack a whip.

Because I had developed excellent relationships with my employees throughout the years, when they did something out of line and I disciplined them about it, we would meet with their shop steward (union shop), and I would provide them the written discipline, I'd shake their hand, smile, and leave. As I left I would say, "I know this will not happen again" and I'd walk out of the room.

The shop steward would look at the employee and ask if she wanted to grieve the discipline and the employee almost always said, "No, I deserved it." The shop steward would come up to me afterward and say, "You know, all the other managers, people would grieve them when they think they need to, but nobody ever wants to grieve when it's your discipline. Why is that?"

Now I didn't ever want to tell him, but the truth is the relationships I maintained with my employees were built on respect and honesty and, as a result, there was no reason for them to grieve anything because they were always going to be treated fairly and respectfully and they knew it.

Okay, so now we return to listening and responding appropriately. I think it's really important that whether it's in managing in general or listening specifically, you need to be respectful and honest in order to be effective in your communication. So when listening, consider the value in what others are saying. Acknowledge the value, ask questions to clarify, ask questions about items of interest. The point is to demonstrate that you are listening and understand the speaker.

Reflection

1. How would you rate your listening ability based on the concepts you just read?

2. Which of the pseudo-listening challenges poses the greatest barrier for you?

3. Where do you see the need to pick up your listening game? With whom? Which of the five points?

CHAPTER TEN

EMPATHY NOT SYMPATHY

Empathy is the ability to understand and share the emotions that another person is feeling. You might think that's a little odd. I'm not suggesting that as a manager that you get all touchy-feely with your employees. I want you to recognize that human beings have this need to connect with other human beings. The most powerful communicators have the ability to connect with the person who they are talking with or listening to. The reason why they're so darn powerful is that they can connect on several different levels, with language, logic, and emotion.

Does this mean that every conversation should be a therapy session? No. That's not what I'm talking about. I just want you to recognize that when you're speaking to employees, realize that they have hopes and dreams, they have fears, and they have secret wishes. They have all sorts of things that you do not have access to unless you can connect with them.

Mirrors

The real secret of effective leadership and effective communication is that the relationship you form, this trust-based, integrity-based relationship that you have with your employees, gives you access to their discretionary effort. We've talked about that before. Discretionary effort is the thing that is the Holy Grail for the people who talk about engagement. How do we get that? It's through relationships, and a relationship starts in this thing called communication.

Let's come back to this concept of empathy. Psychologists tell us we have mirror neurons in our brains.[18] These have been associated with the development of empathy. Essentially this is a cognitive process—when a person observes another's actions, the first person can mimic the brain activity of the second person, and hence literally feel the same emotion. When a person speaking sees that someone listening to them is demonstrating empathy, the speaker can actually feel listened to.

In his book *Just Listen*, psychologist Mark Goulston argues that some people suffer from a mirror neuron deficit, meaning that there aren't enough people in their lives who are actually mirroring what they are feeling; that they don't feel listened to.[19] Really this is a remarkable thing, because if you can get to the point where your employees feel like you are listening, they will give you the discretionary effort.

So, how do we get there from here? You're thinking, *Ron, I'm not a psychologist.* I'm here to tell you that you don't need to be one: you just need to have empathy. The good news, ladies and gentlemen, is that it's not that complicated—I will show you how. The first thing is that you have to be aware, pay attention, and demonstrate authentic curiosity.

We talked about listening in the last chapter. Active listening will give you the information you need to begin developing empathy. When people speak, you don't want to just listen to the words they say; you want to listen to the tone level too.

Once you are able to recognize the different emotions behind the words, you can mirror back or reflect that emotion to them. "Wow, that must make you really frustrated." "Wow, it sounds like you're angry about that." "Wow, if that happened to me I'd be so upset." Whatever the phrase is, all you've got to do is mirror or reflect that emotion back to them in a way where they can say, "Yeah, you're right. I am." Something really funny happens when you feel listened to: it helps you breathe. As Mark Goulston says, "when they breathe, they can listen to us."[19]

Authentic Curiosity

For me, the concept of empathy begins with authentic curiosity. It's so funny, because every now and again I deal with a manager or an employee who looks at me and says, "But, Ron, I don't care about anybody else. I don't want to know them. I'm not curious about them."

Let me offer you a little tactic that you can use if you struggle with this. As a coach, I listen to people all day long. There are times when somebody is telling me a story and I'm just not feeling it. I'm not connected to it. I have this clear strategy to find something in what they're saying that is of interest to me, even if it's only remotely interesting, and I'll ask them an open-ended question about that thing. It doesn't take them off of the path they're on. It just gives them the opportunity to go deeper in an area of what they're sharing that's also interesting to me and allows me to reconnect.

That to me is authentic curiosity. It's the ability to be curious about your employee. Recognize that your performance is directly dependent on them anyway, so the better you get to know them, the more you understand what motivates them. Through listening to them, the more curious you'll be, and the better your performance is. It's that simple.

The other thing that you need to do is consider your sensitivity to demonstrated emotion. There is a form of pseudo- listening, where we seek to reduce the tension that's starting to build between us and the other person. We might change the subject, crack a joke, or make an offhand remark. I want you to recognize how damaging that can be if somebody is starting to reveal a little bit of an emotional state to you. If you crack a joke, you shut him down and he will never come back, so be careful with this.

If he's demonstrating some emotion, I want you to have enough sensitivity to recognize it, name it for him, and then let him breathe. I guarantee you, after that the conversation will change. He'll go deeper, he'll be listening to you, and you'll be able to start talking about performance, so empathy is really important.

Here's a fun exercise you can try the next time you have a small group together. I use a version of this often in my training classes as a team-building exercise.[20]

You arrange everyone in a circle and say, "We're going to take turns sharing something we're passionate about. We'll each have thirty seconds." Then I hand everyone a recipe card with a letter of the alphabet on it. Each person holds their card out so everyone can see which letter they have.

After everyone has had a turn, I collect the index cards, shuffle them, and hand them back out (making sure the person doesn't get their own card). Then I ask, "All right, who's got A?" Someone responds, "I've got it over here." I ask, "What did the person who had A last time say? What was the core message?" It's a listening exercise on the first pass and most people do fairly well.

The next level is what I really want you to focus on. Once everyone has had a turn, I pick up the cards again, shuffle them, and hand them out randomly a second time, again making sure that nobody repeats a card. Now

I say, "This time who has A? The person who had A the first time, not the second time, what was their core message? What was their theme, twenty-five words or less, and how do you think it made them feel?"

What happens, ladies and gentlemen, is that you'll start to try to name the emotion and the other person, if you name them, they'll be nodding and smiling and going, "Yeah. You got it." If you're way off base, they'll be kind of looking at you with this quizzical look and a furrowed brow saying, "No. That's not it."

It's a really powerful little exercise that will help you grow in your ability to name emotions and recognize them while they're being shared. Try it out to help you grow in your empathy.

Reflection

1. How empathetic are you? How would your employees rate you?

Part 3/Tools for Performance

CHAPTER ELEVEN

SETTING CLEAR EXPECTATIONS

Before I talk about how to set expectations, I want to spend just a minute talking about why this is so important and make sure we're on the same page. In my years of management, I have discovered that there are certain basic things that, if we do them exceptionally well, will lead to higher performance. This is, by all accounts, probably the easiest thing we could possibly do to create high performance: setting clear expectations. The biggest roadblock with expectations is our assumptions. We think that because we've actually told an employee, "Here's what I expect of you, go do this" or we've given them a project and said, "Here's your deadline," we think we've done a good job of setting expectations.

Well I've got news for you . . . AAAHHH, you didn't do it right! Hate to be so abrupt with you, but you really need to hear this. One of my favorite authors is management expert Ken Blanchard. I was reading some work on his website one day and he related this story: he went into a number of different organizations and talked to 1,400 leaders. In his research he found that the top two mistakes managers make relate to feedback and expectations. A full 82 percent fail to provide useful feedback about performance and redirection to employees.[21]

In another study by the Blanchard organization, they found a 28 percent gap between what employees wanted in performance-standard setting and expectations and what was experienced.[22] No wonder employees don't always know what's expected of them!

Challenge #1—send clear messages: Many of us are not good at deliberately setting expectations, and even when you think you are, the employee often hasn't heard you. That is because we tend to share it in a way that's expedient to us. Maybe we send an email, maybe we just were talking off the cuff while we were walking to another meeting. We're the manager, they're supposed to listen, right? Employees don't always hear what we tell them.

Challenge #2—the listening problem: Recall the perceptual position model discussed earlier in this book. Employees are focused on their own needs; they're not necessarily focused on what we need but focused on what they need. As a result, if you don't make the effort to ensure they're listening to you in the moment, chances are they won't hear you.

Is it any wonder that in marketing they say that you need at least seven points of contact with a customer before the customer actually remembers your brand? When it comes to setting expectations and communicating with employees, it's no different. The challenge is that unless you're thinking about how they're listening to you (or whether they're listening to you), the amount of contact and the number of words you're using has little pertinence as to how well they hear you. You need to be considering whether they are actually listening and take steps to make sure they are, as we discussed earlier.

Challenge #3—the speaking problem: The next challenge is the speaking problem. We, as managers, speak quite often. The way we speak isn't always tailored to the needs of the employee. In fact, it's thinking about things from our own point of view, not the point of view of the employee. What's this got to do with anything? As you set an expectation based on manager speak, as I like to call it, you might start talking about return on investment, capital asset allocation, internal rates of return, and all the terms that you use in senior levels of management. What does the employee know about those things? You've got to watch the language that you use to make it understandable for the employee.

You've got all these challenges that are working against you as it relates to employees understanding what's expected of them. Let me build one other point of view in this matter. I'm a fond follower of the Gallup organization. I read much of what it has to say about the concept of engagement. I find the work to be brilliant.

Gallup organization researchers have created an employee engagement survey. There are twelve questions that they claim are predictive of employee engagement (on a scale of 1 to 5 with 1 meaning completely disagree and 5 meaning completely agree). Gallup, in all its work, has identified the importance of setting clear expectations for employees to be engaged. If the employees don't know what they're doing, they can't do it right.

Let's look at the questions and how they relate to setting expectations:

Question 1: I know what is expected of me at work.

Question 2: I have the materials and equipment I need to do my work right.

Question 3: At work, I have the opportunity to do what I do best every day.

[Author note: How can employees do their best if they don't know what it's supposed to be?]

Question 4: In the last seven days, I have received recognition or praise for doing good work.

[Author note: How can employees know and do their best if they don't know that they've done their best? In an upcoming chapter we're going to discuss the power of feedback. Question 4 absolutely relates to this. You need to let your employees know, after you've set the expectation, how they're doing. More on that one in an upcoming chapter.]

Question 5: My supervisor, or someone at work, seems to care about me as a person.

[Author note: I want you to recognize, whether you are a task-oriented manager or relational manager by nature, how important it is for employees to feel like they matter, feel like they're making a contribution. The best person to do that is you. One of the things that I've often heard about organizational culture is that it isn't some grand thing that a person from human resources comes up with and puts on a website.

Culture is what employees experience from you, their manager. What's the culture of your organization from the employee's point of view? Is it a caring environment? Is it a challenging environment? Is it an abrasive, coercive, fear-based environment? What is it? Question 5 is important to answer this topic.]

Question 6: There is someone at work who encourages my development.

[Author note: Someone wants the employees to do their best. What a powerful statement. Again, how can they do their best if they don't know the expectations and are not encouraged to go after it?]

Question 7: At work, my opinions seem to count.

[Author note: Let me tell you, listen to your employees. That's the answer to this one. My opinion counts because my manager makes me feel like he or she cares. He or she really listens.]

Question 8: The mission or purpose of my company makes me feel my job is important.

[Author note: Here it is again. People want to make a difference. They want to know that they matter. The first step in knowing that they matter is setting clear expectations. If you want to make it just a little bit better, connect the expectations of their roles to the mission and purpose of the company.]

Question 9: My associates or fellow employees are committed to doing quality work.

[Author note: This question is kind of a funny one. From my experience, this is the question that gets hammered because employees always want their coworkers to perform at a high level, especially if they're a performer. I'll tell you what. Taking care of this question requires intestinal fortitude to hold people accountable and to challenge them to be their best and to develop relationships to help them actually achieve their best. Nine is an important question.]

Question 10: I have a best friend at work.

[Author note: This should speak volumes to the fact that people spend the best hours of their day at work. They want to be around people who they like, trust, and respect.]

Question 11: In the last six months, someone has talked to me about my progress.

[Author note: If you haven't talked to the employees in the past seven days, you get it in question 11. Have they talked to you in the past six months?]

Question 12: This last year, I have had opportunities at work to learn and grow.[23]

To sum up: what you need to recognize is that employee engagement, in particular, and performance, in general, is grounded in this sense of employees feeling like they matter; feeling like they're challenged to do their best; feeling like someone cares about them; and feeling like they're getting communicated with, listened to, and talked to in a collaborative and respect-based environment.

I want you to recognize Gallup question 1, "I know what is expected of me at work." It's that important. If your employees don't know what's expected, they can't do their best, they won't be engaged, and you live in mediocrity land, okay?

You've bought into the idea that you've got to set clear expectations so the next obvious question is: how do you do it?

First point: talk one-on-one. Giving employees expectations in a group session might be expedient for you but it is not effective for them unless every employee has exactly the same expectations. For those of you who are dealing with operational roles, where there are many people in the same position, perhaps it works. Even then, I still recommend you talk one-on-one to clarify and make sure the employee understands. If it's a unique position that only one person does, it's critical that you provide one-on-one communication.

Second point: You need to spend some time making sure that you completely understand what the expectations are in the first place and that you can relate them to the organization's purpose and mission. It's a strategic piece of management but it's really critical. It gets to those Gallup questions I just talked about. Employees want to know that their contributions are meaningful. Make sure that you understand the expectations, you can speak to them intelligently and clearly, and you can link them to the importance in the organization.

Third point: Encourage your employees. When you're communicating one-on-one and explaining expectations, encourage the employees to write the words down and repeat them back to you. You might say, "Well, I sent an email. They already got it, why should they write it? That seems like a waste." Well, okay, I respect your opinion; however, I'm going to respectfully disagree with your opinion because here's the thing. There's a part of our brain, when we write things down—even if we never go back and look at it again—writing it down embeds it in our memory in a deeper way that greatly improves the probability that we'll actually follow through and meet that expectation.

Writing it down and repeating it back, helps embed it in the employees' memory, helps make it more likely that they will actually live up to it. Another thing, as you're considering the expectations of each employee, you want to make sure that the expectations are specific enough, that they're clear, that they're measurable, so the employees know when they're complete and they can communicate to you when they're finished.

Expectations should have a deadline if they're goal oriented. If they're behavioral expectations, this is the way we talk to one another, obviously there's no deadline. Anything that's task oriented should have a clear deadline. Deadlines are one of the most powerful motivating forces in goal theory. Just make sure that they're specific, measurable, and timed.

After-Action Review

Another aspect of setting expectations is teaching your employees how to deal with missing an expectation or underachieving. One of my favorite ways to do this is something called an after-action review. This is a concept that comes out of the US military where when a mistake is made or an objective's missed, the **first step** is to ask, "What happened?" You're looking for an objective— just a statement of facts, no opinions or emotions.

In an after-action review, you want to remain as objective as possible. It's hard for a human being to be completely objective. We tend to be subjective in the way that we think. One of the best ways to eliminate subjectivity when you're answering the question, "What happened?" is to outlaw the concepts of blame and shame. I do that, personally, because they rhyme. When I say, maintain objectivity, what I'm saying is don't blame people, just look at what actually happened. Separate the fact of what happened from your subjective meaning that you assign to it.

The **second step** and next questions are, "Why do you believe it happened? What are the root causes of this event?" In the process of root-cause analysis, you first have to define what you're going to base root-cause analysis on. The challenge with root-cause analysis is it's really a delicate process to separate your objectivity from your subjectivity. In fact, often in root-cause analysis, subjectivity is going to come in no matter how hard you try to keep it out. My thought about no blame and no shame is a clear boundary that I try to keep—boundary condition—to keep people in the objective.

If you can understand the root causes, then you can move on to the **third step**, which is to ask, "How do you keep it from happening again?" What you're looking for are behavioral changes on the part of the employees that they can make to ensure that next time there's a higher probability of achievement. Having a model allows them to know that, while it's not okay to miss, it's important to keep learning.

So you've met expectations . . . now what do you do? You need to follow up on their follow though. If they don't come back to you and let you know that they've achieved the expectation, you definitely want to be connecting with them to find out where they are in the process. In fact, if you want to be proactive and really help people grow, make sure that you get with them *before* the deadline so they have just enough time to work on it, if they're a bit of a procrastinator. This doesn't have to be as onerous as it sounds.

There are so many different time-management tools embedded in technology today where you can set yourself reminders a week in advance to check on an employee's progress. These are just a few of the ways in which you can provide your employees with clear expectations about what is expected of them.

Behavioral Expectations

Employees also need to be able to interact successfully with other employees. Here are some thoughts on setting behavioral expectations. You can start by taking a look in the mirror. Do not set behavioral expectations that you're not prepared to follow yourself or you're setting yourself up for failure. Integrity demands that you walk your talk, not be a hypocrite—do as I say, not as I do. That's something you have to deal with and make sure that your standard is one that you will hold other people accountable to and you'll also hold yourself accountable to.

Next look at what it means to treat people with dignity and respect. What level of disagreement will you deal with or tolerate within an organization? How do you want to disagree? One of my favorite quotes from Dr. Peter Drucker, a management consultant and developer of the Drucker MBA program at Claremont Graduate University is this: "Conflict is two people in a room together." I think that's absolutely true, that if you get two people together, they'll find something to be in conflict about. That said, you ought to have clear guidelines about how you're going to deal with the inevitable conflict in ideas, in perspectives, etc.

You want to outline and think proactively about all the likely possible interactions that could go wrong. You want to identify how you do things at the company. Make sure, as I said, that you're setting the example. You want to deal with conflict, you want to deal with communication, and you want to deal with anything else that comes up.

Reflection

1. If I were to ask your employees what your top expectations for them were, how would they respond? Would they give me crisp, quantitative answers? Would they give me a deer-in-the-headlights look or something in between?

2. What steps can you take today to begin ensuring your employees have clarity about what is expected of them?

3. Do you agree that your employees should have clear behavioral expectations? If not, how many conflicts do you plan to referee this week while your employees under-perform?

4. What process do you have in place to ensure your employees learn to adjust to missed expectations? Is it working consistently?

CHAPTER TWELVE

DEALING WITH BEHAVIOR MODIFICATION

Well, there are a number of different ways of handling it when a person's behavior disrupts the workplace. In this chapter I am going to focus on whining and complaining, although you can substitute almost any objectionable behavior. During my training classes, I often discuss behavioral modification with supervisors. You need to recognize that your employees are 20, 30, 40, and 50+ years old. They didn't get that way overnight. It took them 20, 30, 40, or 50+ years to get there. What in the heck makes you think you're going to change them with one piece of feedback and one request to change? It doesn't work that way.

The thing about whiners is that they didn't start whining yesterday. They probably started a decade ago and they've continually felt unheard and so they amp it up in an effort to be heard over the noise of the workplace. Some whining you can correct with listening, absolutely. When they feel listened to they're going to be less likely to complain, but those are the employees who are somewhat aware that they're whining and they understand that complaining is a bad behavior.

However, what do you do if they're so entrenched in that behavior that they don't even realize that they're whining? (Trust me, there are people who don't realize that they're whining.) You will need to take a more intensive approach and this might include direct feedback, such as telling them, "When you behave that way, people tend to tune you out. What do you think you could do differently?" They might respond, "Well, I guess I could stop whining and complaining, but that's not fair." You build awareness by reminding them that they're still whining.

Let me give you an example of this. I was working with a logistics organization a few years back and training the front-line employees. The group I was working with represented a challenge for the management staff. This group had seniority and a strong sense of entitlement that wasn't being filled. I recall in one class, a member of the team started complaining that management wasn't listening to their complaints, taking no positive actions. I asked this person what exactly they wanted done. They wanted to be listened to. I told the person that I had indeed heard them and that I would relay their comments to the management team. They seemed satisfied with this and agreed my action would address their complaint. I did share it with their manager shortly afterward.

In a follow-up class, the same person started complaining about the same issue. Halfway through the comments, I politely stopped her and said, "Hold on a minute, this is the same comment you made last time we met. I listened to you then, and shared it with management as I promised. You agreed that this would satisfy your concern. Why are you bringing the same issue up that you agreed you would not?"

This person was dumbfounded. I don't think they had ever been held accountable for their comments before in this way. Holding them accountable in this forum did not damage our relationship and it set the right standard for self-responsibility in communication.

Somebody can't change a behavior that they're not conscious of producing. If they are not aware of how they're behaving and how it's received, they can't change it. They just don't realize that they're even doing it. All learning starts from a place of ignorance or when you're unconscious of your incompetence in a specific skill set. It's only when we become aware of the incompetence that we're demonstrating or even our ability to communicate, that we need to make a choice to do something about it.

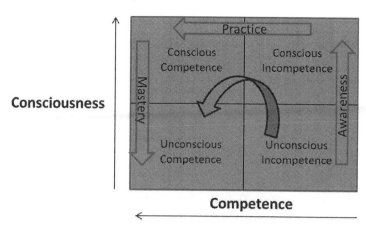

Learning and coaching model[24]

The choice is to either remain ignorant or to move to a place where you realize you need to improve. Now you've got to practice a new skill. When you practice a new skill, you are now conscious of your incompetence, and the more you practice it, the better you get; you become consciously competent.

The way we move to mastery is we practice it, and practice it, and practice it, and eventually we get so good at it we no longer need to think about it. It's similar to learning how to ride a bicycle. How would you teach somebody who grew up in a remote village in the Amazon and had never seen a bicycle before? Would you hand him a bicycle and say, "Here, have a ride"? They have no context for it. How about this? You go up to him and say, "Have you ever ridden a bicycle?" They're going to look at you and go, "What's a bicycle?" They have no conscious knowledge of what you're talking about. They can't possibly know.

Unconscious incompetence and awareness building leads to conscious incompetence, practice leads to conscious competence and repeated practice leads to mastery and hence, unconscious competence. That's the way we learn and the whiners are generally not conscious of the fact that they're whining. The first step is to make them aware of it. Potentially, if they're really entrenched, you might need to make them aware of the consequences of continued behavior so that they understand that there's a price to be paid within your organization if they continue to alienate people and under- perform.

As they become aware of it now, they might seek a change of behavior. They're starting to think about how they talk about subjects and are wondering if people are thinking they're whining, and that is a good thing because now they're actually censoring the way that they approach their communication. The more they do it, the better they get.

Now I have talked about behavior modification using the example of a whiner. The same approach is applicable to almost all behaviors you want to help your employees modify.

In the next chapter, we will connect behavior modification to the delivery of performance feedback, which is a critical tool in helping employees to improve and ultimately to improving organizational performance.

CHAPTER THIRTEEN

PROVIDING FEEDBACK

In an earlier chapter, we talked about a basic model of communication and we discussed how communication doesn't occur unless you have an effective feedback loop and you know that the person understood you in the first place. The way that we approach giving feedback is absolutely critical. In this chapter, we will talk about a different form of feedback, performance feedback.

I want to give credit to two sources that have done some excellent work in this area. First, is the Center for Creative Leadership (CCL.org).[25] it has a basic model of how to give performance feedback that I think is absolutely fantastic. In the model, it's simple. **First,** you need to be able to describe the situation where the employees performed in a certain way or did not perform in a certain way. You need to be able to describe the situation to them. **Second,** you need to be able to describe their behavior. There is a lot of nuance to describing behavior that we are going to dig into about how to give feedback. **Third,** you want to describe the impact to you, using I-statements. We're going to build on this in order to create a model of how to give feedback.

There are two management consultants that I have a tremendous amount of respect for whose names are Mike Auzenne and Mark Horstman. They run a consultancy and have a website by the name of Manager Tools.[26] They teach a model that builds on CCL's work and has two added steps. The first is about permission and the final step is about next steps. We'll build on the groundwork of these two organizations.

So, what is effective feedback? In my training classes, I love to start the conversation on feedback in a simple way. Imagine you board a plane at LAX on your way to LaGuardia in New York City. The plane takes off on its way to New York. What percentage of the time do you think the plane is headed directly toward New York City? Like absolutely on point of the compass in the exact right direction? People think this is a trick question. They say, "Oh, clearly 95 percent. It's got to be headed there mostly the whole time, doesn't it?" Actually no, it doesn't. When you factor in air traffic control, traffic patterns and the jet stream, the pilots are rarely directly headed on an exact path toward New York.

They will actually take slight deviations in the flight path one way or another based on the guidance that they're given until they arrive at their destination. How do they manage to do it? Most people assume, "Well, they have autopilot." Sure they do. But what is autopilot? Usually at this point, people in the training class begin to recognize the point I'm trying to make. They say, "Oh, well there are instruments and the devices in the cockpit of the jet that actually measure things that get them there. Oh. So you're actually measuring things like direction, wind speed, and altitude and all these different factors."

In essence, the airplane is getting real-time feedback about its position and that feedback is absolutely critical for it to arrive at its destination. Now the light bulbs come on and folks understand, "Okay. So a plane needs feedback. What's that got to do with me as a manager?" Well, it has everything to do with you as a manager because your employees need feedback in order to perform.

Let me give you a simple example that I love to do in my training class. I ask for two volunteers: one person performs as the supervisor, the other person as an employee. I give them a simple exercise and I say, "Miss Employee. We want you to count 10 seconds, five times in a row. I'm going to say start and then stop. Your supervisor is going to measure your performance." I set out a cell phone in front of them with a timer. When you say start, they start the clock. When you say stop, they stop the clock.

I whisper to the supervisor, "All right. For the first five measurements, give absolutely no feedback. Keep a straight face. Don't look at her. Just record the data."

So they go through five times and inevitably what happens when you do this is that the "employee" will be at seven seconds, nine seconds, twelve seconds, six seconds, or eight seconds. They're all over the clock, and I ask them at the end, "So how did you do?" "Well, I don't know."

I say, "What do you mean you don't know? You're the expert at the job. You're supposed to be able to do this incredibly well. I pay you to get results.

How did you do? Well, would it surprise you to know that you did extremely poorly and I need you to pick up your performance?"

You see? This is exactly how many managers give feedback: incorrectly. They expect the employees to know exactly how to perform when they haven't gotten any feedback about how they performed in the first place.

In the next step of the exercise, I have the two people repeat their roles except this time I instruct the "supervisor" to offer only negative feedback. Each time the "employee" stops below 9½ or more than 10½ seconds, I tell them to shake their head or make a tsk-tsk sound, indicating their displeasure. Eventually the employee becomes self-conscious and frustrated.

So we finish the five sets. I look at them and say, "Well, why didn't you get it done this time? You were given feedback." They say, "But I don't know how I did." I have had some people hang their head in embarrassment, others dig in, narrow their eyes, and resolve to try harder. Others get nearly belligerent and start arguing with me.

The third time I have the supervisor give the employee specific performance feedback to tell them exactly how they did each time. And the people in the class get it—real feedback creates real outcomes and improves performance. So the point is that performance feedback is the most fundamental aspect of management.

You've got to let your employees know how they're performing. I was able to use this in a previous management role with an under-performing group to actually rocket their quality score up to the standard within three months and keep it there for almost four years because they knew how they were performing, among other things. Performance feedback is that fundamental.

If you accept my argument that performance feedback is absolutely critical to success, then the most important question might be: "So why don't we give it?" The truth of the matter is it's not often done well and when it is, it isn't done often enough. There are many reasons that I believe that managers don't give feedback.

First, we're not skilled at providing it and because we're not particularly skilled at providing it, what often happens is that conflict occurs. As we don't want to get in a conflict situation, we eventually stop giving feedback. And the reason we get into conflict is because we don't know how to give feedback. It's a vicious cycle! But what if it were easy to give feedback? Wouldn't you do it more often? I'm hoping your answer is yes because it really is the most fundamental thing that a manager needs to know how to do well.

I follow a simple five-step model that, as I mentioned, comes from a mix of the work of the Center for Creative Leadership and Manager Tools.[27]

The first step is permission.

The second step is the situation or context.

The third step is the behavior.

The fourth step is the impact.

The fifth step is next steps.

As we walk through the model I'm going to show you how to use it in three ways. The first is for when you're talking to your employee, the second is how to provide feedback to peers and, finally, how to give your manager or supervisor feedback. I have to warn you right out of the gate that giving your supervisor feedback is a dangerous thing to do. So I want you to be careful and pay attention when we get to that model.

Employee Feedback

Let's start with the first step; **permission.** You want to start out with a question and I love the way that Mark Horstman from Manager Tools says it. He suggests that giving feedback should be as effortless as breathing and I couldn't agree more. First, what type of feedback do you think the average employee gets throughout his or her career? There are basically three possibilities: positive, neutral, or negative. What kind of feedback do you think most employees have gotten? If you answered anything but negative, I think you're probably a little bit idealistic.

Most employees are accustomed to getting negative, critical, hurtful feedback and, unfortunately, the minute you start talking about feedback, up goes the defensive barrier. Do you remember the perceptual position model we talked about? The first position was about focusing on self-need. When we feel threatened, whose interests do you think we focus on? So if you say, "Hey, I've got to give you some feedback" or "Come to my office. I need to give you some feedback." Guess what? The employee starts to get worried because he expects something bad to happen. He drops into first position and up goes the defensive barrier. And he will not be listening to you! But it doesn't have to be that way!

PERMISSION: I prefer to ask permission to give feedback because it will deflect the defensive reaction the average employee might respond with; if a person can remain open, he has a better possibility of listening to you. Another reason to ask permission is because you don't necessarily know the state of mind of another person. If he's not in the right frame of mind and you pile on, you just never know what could happen.

Technically, you need to be a little more sensitive to the fact that your employees might not be in a good place to accept feedback and if they're in a bad place, I have a simple suggestion for you. Don't give them feedback at that moment.

Now, you might be thinking, *Does that mean I'm not going to give feedback? That takes away all my power.* The short answer: no. The long answer: I encourage you to ask for permission to give feedback the next day. If they say no again, then it gives you an opportunity to have a conversation. You might ask, "What's going on with you?"

You might realize that the performance that you're trying to give them a feedback about was influenced by some external factor that you're not aware of. Once you're aware, you now have options available to you. You can get them into your employee assistance program or connect them with human resources and help them with whatever they're dealing with so they can actually perform for you again. This is a win-win. If they say no to you three times, the conversation changes. Now you have to give them some feedback about not accepting feedback. See? Performance feedback is so critical to employee performance.

It's not their right to not accept it, but it is their right to accept it at a time that will work better for them.

Which brings me to another objection that I often hear. You know how sometimes managers think they're all that and a bag of chips or they're a little bit too macho for their own good? They're a little bit too aggressive. You know that type of person? Right about now they're probably thinking, I don't need this. *I don't need to ask my employees' permission. I should be able to just tell them. I'm in charge.*

Well, I'll tell you what. How about you get over yourself and recognize that you're not giving away power by asking a person this question. You're not negating any aspect of your managerial role. What you are doing is simply respecting the other human being that's in the employee-manager relationship with you and, by doing this, you create a more effective relationship where they will actually want to perform for you. It's just a subtle little thing. Asking the question is a respect-based decision. Asking permission is really critical.

SITUATION: The situation for me is simply: What was going on? Where did you see them? What was happening at the time? Describe the scene. Describe the context. Describe the background. You want to let them know that you saw something and are addressing it.

In my training classes I am often asked, "Should I give feedback based on somebody else's observations?" Be really careful with this! My advice is no. Imagine a fellow manager comes to me and says, "Your employee did this." Would I give you feedback on that? No, I wouldn't. I would actually take a specific approach. With that other manager, I'd say, "Thank you very much. I'll keep an eye out and if I see it too, I'll give them feedback." What do you think would be a natural reaction of an employee if you told them someone had seen them texting? They want to know, "Who said that?" Now you have just started a witch hunt. You just started to pit one employee against another in an incredibly unhealthy, conflicting kind of way and you're making them paranoid of their peers.

Give feedback on what you see. The cool thing is that when you give feedback on what you have seen, you know what? They can't fight it. They can't say that they didn't do it because now they're calling you a liar and they work for you and they respect you. They will not call you a liar. Recognize the power of seeing it for yourself. Once you've decided to give feedback on something you've seen, then you describe the situation. Tell them what you saw, in detail. This leads us into the next step, behavior.

BEHAVIOR: This is really the heart of effective feedback and the reason that most managers don't like to give it. The reason that they get into conflict when they give feedback is that they haven't mastered the concept of behavior. They think they have, but they haven't. Let me ask you a simple question. Is a bad attitude a judgment or behavior? If you said it was a behavior, you're wrong. Bad attitude is our judgment of a series of behaviors that an employee has demonstrated that we have put together and said when somebody does X, Y, and Z, they have a bad attitude.

Now, exactly what can employees do about a bad attitude? Do you expect them to walk around smiling all the time looking goofy? You need to focus on the behavior. So, the definition of behavior that I like to work from is simple. What can I see? What can I hear? What can I measure? So, if an employee misses a deadline, that's a measurable outcome that is worthy of feedback. If an employee rolls their eyes and sighs when somebody's talking or cracks a joke and giggles when someone else is speaking, that is a behavior. If an employee misses a production quota, that is behavior. If an employee has errors in his administrative work, that is a behavior. You see? You've got to be able to see it, hear it, or measure it. Now, let me go a little deeper with this. This is really a critical point and you can actually do this.

At this point in a training class, I'll instruct the people to watch a video clip. I'll tell them to pay attention to what they see because after the video we'll make a list of behaviors. After they've viewed the clip, I'll go to the whiteboard and say, "Okay, what'd you see?"

I take a red marker and begin to write. Someone will say, "He was listening," so with a red pen I'll write on the whiteboard: listening. The next person might say, "He was very confident," so I write in red: confident. Eventually someone will say, "She made eye contact," and I'll write in green: eye contact. The next suggestion might be, "I saw him smile." I write smile in green.

Why red versus green, you might ask? Red is a judgment, green is a behavior: once you can separate the two, something really powerful happens in the feedback process. When I focus on a behavior, it is a fact. Not a judgment, a fact. If it's a fact that you have personally seen, the employee cannot argue with you. If they can't argue with you, then they're faced with the reality of a negative behavior and now they have a choice to make, which is exactly where we go with impact.

If it's a positive behavior, what we want to do is reinforce it. But if you give them a judgment, up goes the defensive wall. They drop into first position. They start to self-protect and most important, they stop listening to you. So, if they stop listening, how effective is feedback going to be? Yeah, you guessed it. Not at all. You need them to be listening.

So the process of feedback is really about a conversation where there is meaning being transferred. It's not about you, Mr. Manager. It is about the employee being able to change his behavior. If you don't address the behavior, you're going to face the same problem again and that's not where you want to go. It's critical that you get into the behavioral level and give your employees the behavior that you want to see changed or the behavior that you want to see more of. When you do that, you help the employee perform. Don't give feedback on judgment—it hasn't worked for you in the past and it won't work for you in the future. Give feedback on behavior. I want you to really hear me say the following sentence.

*An employee **cannot** change your judgment of them.*

*An employee **can** change the behavior that led to your judgment.*

IMPACT: This is the step when you address the consequences of behavior. It could be something as simple as, "When you sigh and roll your eyes when so-and-so is talking, it undermines the effectiveness of our team. You could start to drive a wedge between us and create conflict." It could be something as serious as, "When you make repeated mistakes like this, it impacts our external customer. It puts our entire business in jeopardy." I don't recommend that you turn it into some big drama and go overboard, but the employee needs to understand that there's a consequence to the behavior.

There is an impact here, so employees need to understand so there's a motivator to change their behavior. Without motivation, they're not going to change, but they need to understand the impact so that they can judge the need for change. If you're providing positive feedback, (which by the way, I recommend you do it at least five times more frequently than negative feedback or corrective feedback), the model's done. I would recommend that at that point you say, "Well done. Do more of it, would you?" or, "How could you also do this in other areas?" That's the end of positive feedback. If you're giving corrective feedback, we have one last step.

NEXT STEPS: "What can you do differently?" I see manager after manager after manager after supervisor after supervisor after supervisor screw this step up. I think it's really important that you ask employees this question rather than offering them a solution to the problem you are giving feedback about. If you tell them what to do differently, chances are they're not going to buy-in unless they're really afraid of the consequences and even then, they're only going to do it when you are around or they think they're going to get caught. Remember the saying, "when the cat's away, the mice will play"?

However, if you ask, "What can you do differently?" They might come up with something. Guess what? It's now their idea and when it's their idea, there's a much higher possibility they're going to follow it. The ownership is a really key part.

This is one of the most powerful ways for us to build a culture where employees take ownership. It's not giving them the answers, but challenging them to find their own. Now, what if you're thinking, *Okay. But, Ron, my employees aren't very bright. What do I do if they can't find an answer?* Good question. If you've asked them about what they can do differently and they don't know, the next step is to not let them off the hook.

If you really haven't been building them up and helping them develop the confidence to do this well, you might need to break it down for them. The first time you might give them something simple, such as, "Who could you talk to about this to learn more?" or " What could you read?" If the next time you're giving them feedback and they come back to the exact same helpless spot, I would give them feedback on their ability to learn. "Hey, when you come back to me and you expect me to find solutions for you, it makes me wonder if you're committed to learning. What could you do differently?" See? Now it's feedback on the feedback. So it's really critical that you follow a model that allows the employee to perform.

So that's the basic model when giving an employee feedback. You start with permission. "Hey, may I give you some feedback?" Deflects defensiveness and it generally might be a bad time. You don't want to give feedback if it's a bad time.

Describe the situation. What was going on? What did you see of them? Where did you see them? What was going on? Describe the behavior. What specific behaviors did you see?

Recognize the difference between a behavior and a judgment. A behavior is something you can see, you can hear, or you can measure.

Then describe the impact. Don't be overly dramatic here. Just give them the impact of their behavior.

Then ask for next steps if it's corrective.

Now let's look at how to offer peer feedback.

Peer Feedback

I want you now to think about a peer. If you say to peer, "What can you do differently?" and they're really sharp-witted, they might come back and say, "Not talk to you." This model doesn't work with peers, so I actually use a subtle variation that I highly recommend and it's called clarification feedback.

So you still ask permission. "Hey, may I talk to you about something?" Not giving feedback, just asking permission. Describe the behavior you saw. Now, instead of talking about the impact next, what I'd recommend you do is one of two things. If it was positive, thank them. Thank them for what they did. If it was something that you think was negative or insensitive in some way, just question for clarity.

My favorite way to do this is to say, "Hey, I noticed in the meeting today that you talked over the top of me and I don't want to misinterpret that. I want to know what was going on for you." If it was just an instinctive thing and she didn't even realize she was doing it, chances are she is going to apologize and say, "Oh, I got really, really enthusiastic. Didn't realize I did that. Sorry! I'll try not to do it again." No big deal, right?

Now, what if she meant to do it? Yeah. What if she's a jerk who really meant to do it and she says, "Huh, I did? Too bad." So now what you've done is you've opened up a place for a professional conversation about her negative behavior and talk about the culture of the organization.

If that's acceptable in your culture, then you've really got to wonder about your culture. But at least now you have the opening and you have, as it's said in the military, taken a shot across the bow of the other person that you're not going to be walked on that way.

But recognize, this is for your peers, not for your employees or your supervisor. This is only for a peer; somebody who is of equal power, equal status in the organization to you. So, it's a really powerful way to do it and whatever you do, don't act superior! Don't ask, "What could you do differently?" That's arrogant. I don't recommend that at all. So, permission, situation, behavior, and ask questions for clarity.

Upward Feedback

Now, how about if you need to give feedback to your manager? What do you do there? I get asked this question all the time and it scares the crap out of me, to be quite honest. Because if you're unsuccessful, you already know that this is a minefield. If you approach this the wrong way, it could backfire on you so quickly that you won't know what happened to you and you've only got yourself to blame. Every now and again throughout my career, I've had managers say, "Ron, give me some feedback about how I'm performing." And I look at that like, "Oh, crap!" So, first, the two models I've just shared with you do not work and I don't recommend them. If you're talking to your supervisor, your manager, if you are cornered and you absolutely have to give them feedback, my recommendation is to start with something incredibly small and insignificant and see how he handles it. If he overreacts or gets defensive, how do you think he's going to take real feedback? So, be really, really careful with this one.

Now, in many professional organizations, there are 360-degree processes, so make sure that they're being done correctly. That is probably the safest way to give your manager feedback, because it's anonymous. I just want you to be really careful because you can derail your career if you do it incorrectly and what I have observed is that there are numerous managers who really don't have the strength of character or the confidence in themselves or self-efficacy to accept feedback in the way it was intended, in order to help them be better at what they do. Be really careful with this one. Be really careful.

Implementation

Another thing I want you to think about is how to implement feedback into your business. The first and most important thing; start with positive feedback. My recommendation is for the first several weeks, you should give nothing but positive feedback. Why? Because if you go to somebody in week one and say, "Hey, may I give you some feedback?" they're going to be suspicious, maybe a little bit sensitive. Then when they hear positive feedback, they'll be curious and it'll mess with their heads and they're like, "What? I was expecting criticism but I got positive words. That felt good."

All right, week two. "May I give you some feedback?" Positive feedback again. Now you're really messing them up.

Week three; maybe they start to trust you a little bit and start to say, "Hey, maybe this is a good thing." Right? You give positive feedback again to reinforce it.

Week four, you give positive feedback again. What are they doing? They're starting to listen to you and be open to your point of view and somewhere in week four, five, or six, somewhere in that time frame, you start to add in small corrections. Not big ones, but something along the lines of "Hey, you know, when you show up to meetings five minutes late, it negatively impacts our process and it especially puts everybody on hold until you arrive. What could you do differently?" All right. Something simple. The reply, "Well, I guess I could show up on time." You say, "Okay. Excellent. Can I count on you to do so?" "Yeah. Okay." Done. And then you go back to positive feedback.

See? By starting with positive feedback, you keep them open to it. You get them positioned to appreciate positive feedback, which is, by the way, a great motivational tool. People, when they start getting used to positive feedback, will appreciate it and they will want more.

So, to whom do you give positive feedback? How about everybody? As I've said before, most of us have an in-group and an out-group. There are those people who we love, who we work with really easily, who are fantastic to delegate to. It's just effortless to talk with them. Giving them positive feedback is no problem.

But here's the real opportunity; the out-group—those people who are different from you. They're frustrating. They're hard to talk to. They don't do things in predictable ways. You tend to look at them with suspicion. Maybe you're even thinking that one of these employees isn't right for your organization. Those are the ones who need feedback too. They also need positive feedback. Hold on, you say, "But they don't do anything positive." Really? Nothing? Really?

Okay, well maybe that's what you think. Okay. So then give them positive feedback on the things they do well. What you will find if you do that is that they will start do other things well and you will start to perceive them in a new light. And if they don't, what's the harm? Well, the harm is I gave positive feedback and now I'm going to have to give a negative review. Oh, really? Well, here's a way of looking at that. If you're specific about the behaviors that they did well and they come to you in a performance review and you give them a negative review and they say, "But you said I was doing a great job." You reply, "Well, yeah, in that particular area. Showing up for meetings on time and being a good team player, but there's more to the job than that." You see? They can't hold it against you and that's really the key. You've got to give feedback correctly. If you're giving it correctly, there's no negative. You're giving everyone positive feedback. So you slowly introduce corrective feedback at weeks four, five, and six.

Now, I know what you're thinking. *Wait a minute, Ron. What if somebody does something really bad in week two of this process?* Well, okay, give them feedback. Correct it immediately. I'm not saying be all or nothing. I'm not saying it's got to be 100 percent positive feedback for several weeks. What I'm saying is if you want to build performance through a process of feedback, you will need to overcome prior poor feedback in a patient process. You want to build a feedback foundation but at the same time, you've still got to manage your business.

If somebody does something stupid, then give some feedback and correct it immediately. Don't let it wait. That is the fundamental problem that most people have with feedback: they wait until it's too late and they've built up thing after thing after thing, and then they explode on the employee and all that does is hurt the employee (not to mention your reputation as a manager or supervisor). It doesn't help him or her to perform. We need to recognize the difference between helping and hurting an employee.

The point of feedback is never to hurt. It is always to help. Here again. If you can use the model for employees and the model for peers, I think you're going to start seeing increased performance. I can give you multiple examples of trainees in my class that have gone out and started giving positive feedback and seeing jumps in performance. Not like little, tiny moves, but jumps. So I highly recommend this as a critical tool in communication that will fundamentally transform performance.

GETTING STARTED: I want to take you back to something I said several chapters ago. Someone you have a relationship with is far more likely to accept feedback from you than a stranger, or a wary employee. Do not underestimate the importance of relationship development to the success of the feedback process.

Let me offer an example to emphasize this point. I was teaching a class at a local university several months ago about communication and the power of feedback. In our conversation I was telling the students about the importance of relationship when providing feedback. I said to them, "The next person who walks down the hall, I'm going to invite into the class and give him or her feedback. How do you think it'll go?" They looked at me with that wide-eyed student look as if to say, "You'd do that, Ron?" Yeah, totally, I would. Then they started getting mischievous, when they realized I was serious and they said, "How about that one?"

Eventually two young people walked down the hall. I invited them into the classroom and said, "Hey, how are you doing? I'm Ron Hurst, nice to meet you. And you are?" We exchanged pleasantries and I looked at them and said, 'What would happen right now if I were to give you some negative feedback? How would you behave?" One of the people (a young man) said that he would consider it wholly. My response was to say, "Really? That's a great answer, now tell me what you're really thinking." He said, "I'd wonder what kind of SOB you are to give a stranger feedback about something you know nothing about." I said, "That's exactly my point!" Had that been a real feedback situation, the employee would not have listened or acted on the feedback.

Find somebody who you can practice with. It's really important that you try to get used to this process because what I have found with feedback—either positive or negative—the more you do it, the easier it gets. It will be difficult and uncomfortable at the beginning, sure. Follow the model, focus on behavior, and you will be pleasantly surprised at the outcome.

Reflection

1. How have you dealt with feedback in the past? Has it worked?

2. How often do you provide your employees reinforcing feedback? How about the low performers?

3. Which step in the feedback model do you think will be most challenging for you? Why? What can you do to improve?

CHAPTER FOURTEEN

LISTENING FOR PERFORMANCE: THE POWER OF QUESTIONS

In this book we've talked a lot about effective communication and the importance of the role of listening in the effectiveness of communication. One of the things that most people don't quite get about listening is that it is an active process. In order to be an excellent effective listener or active listener, you need to know how to ask questions. What I want to do is just briefly walk you through some of the different types of questions that you might come across while you are talking to someone. There are four basic styles of questions I want to introduce.

Leading

Sometimes we ask leading questions. These are questions that are designed to get the answer that we think we want to hear. You might say to somebody, "Hey, so wouldn't you agree that this is a good course of action?" If you're an employee and your manager says that to you, you almost can read between the lines that saying yes would probably be a good idea. If you ask a question like that, listen to the way the employees answer it and see if they don't have a little hesitating question mark at the end of their yes. Leading questions are a little manipulative and they will tend to get you the wrong information. Leading questions are one of the reasons why we end up with CEO disease—where everybody tells you what they think you want to hear.

Comparative Value

Another style of question is called the comparative value question. "Which position would you be more interested in, position A or position B?" Imagine you're the employee and your manager is saying something like that to you, and you're interested in position C. Is that even an option to you? Comparative value questions limit choice on the part of the other person, which can be a really dangerous thing to do as they might feel like you're railroading them into a specific outcome that you have already predetermined.

Unlike a leading question, a comparative value question is actually fairly useful when trying to clarify. If your employee says, "Well, you know, I'm interested in maybe going over here in the future or maybe going over there." You then ask, "Which of those two options is more appealing to you in the three-year time frame?" Now you're doing a comparative value but it's based on the information they're giving you in the first place. It's more helpful than manipulative.

Closed Ended

One of the most common questions that a manager likes to ask is a closed-ended question, which is a question that can only be answered with yes, no, true, false, or one of two answers. "Are you committed to our organization?" There are only two options with that question. If you get anything other than a yes or no, you're going to be looking at them like they're strange. These are important questions and great if placed early in a conversation, but you've got to be careful not to use too many of them. The employees can feel like you're trying to drive them down a specific road.

Open Ended

If you really want to understand an employee's point of view, the best and most powerful question is of an open-ended question. "Tell me what you would do in a similar circumstance in this situation I'm facing. How would you approach it?" An open-ended question like that allows your employees to reflect on the question, they can think about it, go a little deeper, and offer you something a little more substantive than just simply a superficial trivial answer that they think you want to hear.

One thing I really want to stress in how you ask questions, is that the way you ask questions is actually conditioning or training your employees about how they sense that you want them to interact with you. If your questions are such that it forces them to think, then guess what? Chances are they're going to think more. If your questions are such that it makes them feel that you just want your own opinion recycled back and they don't need to think, that they just have to agree with you, then that's exactly what you're going to get.

Recognize how powerful asking questions in a certain way can be. Your employees will start to create outcomes for you that you don't even see, over the long term. When you're listening as a manager and you're using the skill of listening to create performance, there are certain ways of listening that I think are important to discuss. What I've observed in most people is they think listening is a passive exercise. As we've already described, there's nothing passive about listening.

I find it is helpful to have a list of powerful questions at my side or in my mind as I'm going through a conversation with an employee. It can significantly influence outcomes for the better. Incorporate the following sets of questions into your conversations and you will begin to see performance results immediately.

Self-Regulation

Have you ever heard the old saying that it takes two to tango? It also takes two to get into conflict. As I said earlier my favorite definition of conflict (by Dr. Peter Drucker) is two people in a room together. We need to be regulating ourselves as we communicate with the other person.

We talked about self- awareness early in this book. When I talk about regulating, what I'm talking about is being aware enough of yourself to actually be able to control how you interact with another human being. Here are some of my most important regulating questions that I've used as a manager in various capacities.

- **What outcome am I looking for here?** I need to have a sense of intentionality in everything I do so that when I engage the employee, I know where I want the conversation to go. It's not like I'm going to jam an answer down their throat, but I at least want to have some clarity about the goal that I'm seeking to achieve.

- **How can I protect my integrity in this moment?** Simply put, without integrity you got nothing. You can't lead people. You're bound to just being a manager and coercing them with your role power. I don't recommend that as an approach, so how can I protect my integrity in this moment? What this means is that you need to be thinking about the promises you're making and whether you can keep them. If you can't, you shouldn't be making them. It's that simple.

- **Am I present right now?** This gets back to that concept of self-awareness. If you can ask yourself that question before you engage (or while you're engaging in conversation), it will help you stay in the moment, even if your brain wants to check out. Another related question is, "Am I listening right now?" When you're in a listening mode, you want to be purposeful in your listening.

- **What perceptual position am I in?** Again, it's related to self-awareness. What am I thinking about, am I focused on my own needs? Am I focused on their needs, so I'm not just an observer speculating on the world around me? Once I know what position I'm in, I can ask myself, Where do I want to be?

- **What am I feeling right now?** Am I angry? Am I frustrated? Am I happy? What emotion am I feeling? If I am in touch with that, I can recognize how it is influencing the behavior and the outward appearance that I'm projecting to the other person.

- **How can I create a win for them right now?** By this I mean I want you to think about your employees. If you can create a win-win, they get something that they want and you get something you want without having to give something up. Isn't that a good outcome? If we started to look at the world that way instead of a win-lose, we need to win and they have to lose, I think you're going to find that resentment stays out of the equation and actual trust starts to build and you'll find yourself able to get more done with that same employee group.

Engaging Others

- **What outcome are you looking for?** What does success look like to you? Often people engage in a conversation that they have not thought through. By asking them that question, you actually set them up to be successful in a conversation and you set yourself up to deal with a lot less frustration. By the way, if you start asking that question on a regular basis of every employee, they'll start asking that of themselves before they come to you.

- **How will this help you?** If an employee comes with a self-serving solution, it will only help them because then the next question once they've identified that, is how does it help the organization? If they can't answer the second question but they answer the first, now you've got a perfect coaching moment where you can say, "You know, everything that we need to do should benefit the organization more than any one individual, so how could you reformulate your solution to benefit the organization first?" Recognize what you've done with those two questions. You have not said no to an employee, shut them down, frustrated, or discouraged them. What you've done is taught them how to think. Set an expectation about how to actually communicate ideas to you.

- **What steps are you willing to take to achieve that outcome?** If they come back to you and say, "Nothing," then you look at them kind of curious and say, "Then why should we do it? You're not committed to it." It's another coaching moment. These questions are powerful coaching questions. Another question in this vein is, "What other options have you considered?"

- **What aspects of your idea are most important to you?** This starts to get at what we're going to talk about in Chapter Fifteen about negotiating. We need to understand what somebody's interests in the situation are rather than their position. Often they come up with these half-thought-out but complete solutions that they think we should just take at their word without any scrutiny and when we start to scrutinize it they start to get hurt, and that doesn't work for anyone. So asking this question is powerful to get out what they really want to see done.

- **What is possible?** Other than that, what is possible? I love to ask this question whenever I hear an employee say, "That will never work!" When you're dealing with negativity, "Hey, what's one positive aspect of this situation?" Then do not let them give you neutral or negative. Force them to go positive. Another way to look at it is, "How can we turn this situation around?" If they're that negative, chances are they don't think about the other side of it. Again, you can start to change the way that they look at things.

- **How can I best communicate with you?** Recognizing that not everybody communicates the same way and asking that question demonstrates a level of respect that you have toward the individual. It shows that you want to try to communicate in a way that works for them.

- **If you were to progress in one area this year, what would you want to accomplish?** Then I kind of joke and say, "Not that you're only going to progress in one, but let's talk about one." I usually ask this question during January and February, as it is goal-setting season. This is a powerful question because now they can dream. They can start to look at their future. Most employees don't know how to do that, so by asking this question you start to give them permission to think about the future.

- **How can we both win here?** Get them also thinking about the win-win.

Why?

We always talk about the five W's and the two H's, who, what, where, when, why, how, and how much. Have you ever thought about those? I think about words often, in particular questions starting with why. Why is an incredibly powerful question starter, but it also is closely tied to an individual's personal motives.

Depending on how you ask a why question, you are as likely to get a defensive, closed response as you are to get a decent answer. I want you to think about what it is you want to hear when you use the word why. Are you looking for blame? Are you looking for a scapegoat? Are you looking to point out an error? If you are, I guarantee you you're going to struggle to get quality answers.

Instead, every why question could be easily turned into a what or a how question. Simply replace, "Why did you do that?" with "What circumstances led to that outcome?" Just changing the wording makes the question a lot more approachable and keeps the defensive barrier down for the employee. I think this is really important that when you're listening to someone that your goal be to get the other person to their best thinking. That best thinking is not going to happen when they get defensive because they're not sure where you're going with your question or if they think you're looking to blame them for something, so be careful with why questions. They are powerful, as I said, but can elicit a defensive response.

If you really want to continue to ask why questions, there's only one other piece of advice I'd offer you, and that is to develop deep, trust-based relationships with all your employees. If you have those, they won't get defensive in the face of a why because they trust you. Nobody reveals his or her true identity unless there's a trust-based relationship present.

The challenge is that people do not give that up freely, especially if they think that the other person can't be trusted with that information or their motives were less than pure. They will protect their motives. It's the last area that we release to another human being. It requires a deep level of trust to really share your hopes, your dreams, your motives, and why you behave the way you do. Not everybody even knows why they behave the way they do.

Let me just offer this perspective. If you were to go up to somebody who you have a long-term relationship with, such as a spouse or somebody you're in a committed relationship with, you can ask them a why question and chances are you'll get a response and it will be an honest response because there's trust. But go up to a stranger, like in a service environment, go the counter and say, "Why did you do that first?" What response do you think you're going to get? Unless you've developed your relationship with that clerk, chances are they're going to get defensive and she'll look at you like, "Who the heck do you think you are to ask me that question?" Employees are kind of between those two extremes.

These are some really powerful questions that you can use when you're in a process of active listening in order to go deeper and discover the best thinking, the best solution, and the best outcomes. Recognize the importance of when employees come up with a good solution and you allow them to implement it without changing it or making it your idea. The likelihood that they will own that outcome goes up substantially, but instead the average manager usually says, "Why don't you just do this," and gives the employee the answer. Now who owns the outcome? The manager does, and the employee will only follow it as long as they feel they have to.

I really want you to think that through and recognize that the power in questions is helping the employees find answers that they will ultimately implement and keep implemented during the long run.

This, as you know, is one of the most challenging things in managing people: keeping the changes changed. The way you ask questions starts to lead to influence. It leads to performance. It leads to relationships and so many different things. I highly recommend that you start to incorporate some of these questions into your communication approach. In the next section, we will examine questions that are powerful when communicating in times of significant problems.

Problem-Solving Questions

Regardless of your functional role, you will encounter problems that need to be solved. This is just a fundamental part of what it means to be a manager. I want to share with you a series of questions that will assist you in approaching problems, such that you can begin to drive to the root cause and ultimately resolution.

- **Where should we begin in defining the problem to be solved?**

  Most rookie problem solvers fail to start in the right place, with a clearly defined problem. As the old saying goes, "If you don't know where you're headed, how will you know when you arrive?" Start problem solving by identifying a clear and simple problem statement that everyone can align with.

- **What would success look like?** As Stephen Covey, author of *The Seven Habits of Highly Effective People*, would say, "Begin with the end in mind."[28] I am regularly surprised how often I encounter people who have not considered what the outcome of their efforts should look like. This question gets to the heart of the issue. I also like to add a warning about this question and add some value to Covey's quote, "Begin with the end in mind—but not with the end defined." Problem solving requires openness to solutions we have not yet found. So be careful not to identify a solution to the problem when stating what success looks like. Rather define success in terms of how a solved problem helps the process involved.

- **What is the objective (and what is the performance standard)?** Be certain that you have clarity about the performance standard you are trying to achieve and where the process was, before you try to solve the problem and improve the process. Often rookie problem solvers are quick to start changing stuff before they clearly measure current performance.

- **What is value to the customer?** No problem-solving activity should be undertaken without first having a clear understanding of how the problem affects the customer. This simple question helps to immediately prioritize problem-solving efforts by raising the priority of those problems that customers care most about.

- **What assumptions have we made?** This is a difficult question to answer, but a critical one to consider. While it might be difficult to see your assumptions before hand, they are often clearly evident after the fact. The good news is we tend to make the same assumptions over and over so if you can identify them after the fact, you can use this knowledge in your next problem-solving activity. The key is to reflect on the entire process of problem solving and identify assumptions made.

- **What barriers can we anticipate?** Identifying potential barriers before you begin problem solving is an important activity to ensure the process stays on track later.

- **What do we know about the process right now?**
- **How can we learn quickly about the process in question?**
- **What in this process is not working reliably?**
- **What are we not controlling in the process that we need to?**

The questions above are designed to help uncover potential root causes. We must listen carefully to the responses as employees might say the right thing in the wrong way, or might be completely off base. It is up to the problem-solving leader to respect the input and discern how to use it wisely.

- **How can we be certain we have addressed the root cause and not a symptom?** This is at the heart of the problem-solving process. Understanding when we have reached the root cause is a difficult yet critical step in ensuring we have actually solved the problem. Here is a hint: if your solution involves further scrutiny or inspection of a process, you have not likely solved the root of the problem.

- **What team structure is optimal to find the solution to this problem?** Some problems require different resources to be solved. Be certain to make sure you have the right experience and skill to actually solve the problem.

- **How can we create buy-in for needed changes?** This is another critical question that must be answered. Leave this one unanswered and expect your problem to come back again as employees go back to "the way we've always done it." This topic was addressed in my previous book, *The First Questions,* in the area of change mastery.[29]

Reflection

1. Which of the questions in this chapter stood out as the one or two you want to practice?

2. Which of the questions seemed unimportant to you? How might you think differently about the question and make it useful?

3. With whom can you practice some of these questions to see just how effective they are?

CHAPTER FIFTEEN

POWER NEGOTIATING

As a manager, you negotiate on a regular basis. I remember one day while I was talking to my general manager he asked me, "What are you doing?" I said, "I'm negotiating." He said, "What do you mean, you're negotiating?" I replied, "Everything is a negotiation." It really stunned him that I would say it that way, but the reality is that everything is a negotiation.

If you go to Starbucks and you want to get a large drip coffee, what are you willing to pay for it? Most of you are thinking, *Whatever is on the price board.* What if I told you that the price board is a suggestion, and it's really just a convention here in North America that says we will pay the price on the board? In other parts of the world, the price is actually a negotiable part of the transaction. Everything we do is a negotiation, whether it's hiring employees or motivating them, trying to get projects done or trying to deal with a customer.

We often look at negotiations and say, "That's what sales people do with customers and it's what purchasing does with suppliers. I don't negotiate anything." Let me tell you, if you change your context about what you think negotiating is from some arbitrary system that purchasing and sales engages in to get the best deal for our company, I think you'll find that negotiation is far more reaching. *Getting to Yes,* by Roger Fisher and William Ury, is an important reference when it comes to negotiation.[30] There are certain terms that Fisher and Ury use in their book that I think are really critical for us to understand as managers. I'm going to talk about a couple of them as I go through this section. It is not my intent to teach you a negotiation class—I recommend that you get Fisher and Ury's book. There are also other great negotiating courses. Karrass[31] also is an excellent resource and offers seminars and training programs about negotiation. What I want you to do is to recognize the core issue of negotiating with people on a regular basis.

We want people to follow the outcomes that we want, and what we find is that they don't always do that, do they? This isn't limited to just your employees. This is family and friends, business colleagues, customers, suppliers, regulators, government officials, even the people who we have conflict with. You want certain outcomes from them.

What we find is that when we actually do the active work of dealing with people, when we're actually in front of somebody trying to negotiate an outcome, we'll realize that it's not some cookie-cutter reality where we can get them to do whatever we want because of our power. In many of these situations, we have no power. We need to learn to get good at negotiating.

Again, at the risk of sounding like a broken record, if you haven't got this by now, you'll realize that I don't believe that we should use our power as a manager in anything but extreme circumstances or when it is absolutely appropriate.

When dealing with employees, if you're dealing with discipline, absolutely use your power. If you're making a hiring decision, a promotional decision, or a merit-rate decision, use your power. However, when it comes to influencing employees to get them to do what you want them to do, do not pull the power card for any other reason than is absolutely necessary. Use influence whenever possible to unlock their discretionary effort to get them to do what you need them to do. I think if you build the relationship, build a trust-based relationship, what you will find is that negotiating actually gets easy. Let me just dispel a common myth about negotiation.

Compromise

The minute I start talking about negotiation in every one of my training classes or in the university courses that I teach, people start talking about the C word—compromise. Compromise to me is a weak solution. What it means is that we're willing to give something up of value to us in order to get something else which is of value to us. I'm not saying there aren't times where compromise is the right approach; I'm saying it shouldn't be our first, go-to approach.

I want you to think about negotiating from a completely different perspective. It's not always a win-lose activity. It might end up there and eventually you might have to compromise somewhere down the line. If the issues are of any importance to you at all, compromise should be your last choice, not your first. Win-lose should be your last outcome, not your first. I want you to go after win-win. In order to create a win-win, you're also going to have to listen to what the other person wants. You need to understand his or her needs.

It's critical that you understand the distinction that negotiation is not about compromise. Compromise is a tactic. Negotiation is a strategy. I think it's really important to differentiate. I want to talk about negotiation, which means that we need to break it down and talk about what a negotiation is. Typically, according to Fisher and Ury, there are three primary areas that we need to consider when we're looking at a negotiation, three domains if you will.

First, it's a substance. What is it that we're trying to negotiate? What is it that we want to achieve? What's at stake? What's being considered?

Second, we need to think about the process. Honestly, this is the part that falls down more often than not in negotiation because we don't have a process. How do you navigate decision making? How do you do that? If you don't intentionally enter into negotiations with a thought of how you're going to progress, you get what you've always gotten, which is mediocrity and frustration and failure. Think about the process. What is the decision-making process going to look like? What does a negotiation process look like?

Third, we also need to be thinking about relationships. The one exception that I would make to what I said about creating a win-win is if you absolutely know that you're doing a one-time transaction, you will never deal with that person again, then perhaps you want to go for a win-lose. However, I'm not saying that's the best strategy. What I'm saying is that it's something to consider. The other thing is what to do if the other person isn't willing to play win-win with you. You've got to protect your interests, don't you? Which means you've got to know what they are.

That gets back to the substance of the negotiation process. I want you to begin to think about negotiation in a different context. It is a win-win process of communication that has the expressed intent of reaching an agreement that both sides can buy into.

The problem with negotiations is that they often fail. Relationships get damaged while time and money are wasted. This need not be the case. I think that what happens within organizations is that we start to build bad blood between two sides of an argument and then it turns into some massive conflict that requires remediation to resolve. It's really difficult to negotiate a win-win outcome when the parties don't trust each other or when there's active conflict operating between both sides. I have been in structured negotiations, situations involving multimillion dollar contracts and this is exactly the reality of those situations. In this situation, I often think that at least one of the sides has an invested interest in maintaining that conflict and a low-trust level in order to create an adversarial relationship. This makes it difficult to get a solution because they think that they need to get a win at the expense of the other side.

How to Negotiate

Have you ever seen a three-year-old toddler in a grocery store with their mother? What do they do when they see a piece a candy they want? They throw a classic temper tantrum. What happens if the mommy gives in and gives the kid the candy? That kid has just learned that when the first answer is no, then what they need to do is throw a temper tantrum to get what they want.

You might ask what the heck that has to do with negotiations. The short answer is everything! Have you ever seen a bully? Have you ever seen a supervisor or a manager who doesn't get what they want? They pound the table, they raise their voice, they berate and belittle, they try to make people feel smaller so they can get what they want. It's the toddler technique. It's an immature way of getting what they want.

How about compromise? I talked a little bit about this before. This is not necessarily a good tactic in a negotiation. At the end, when it's clear that you've made as much progress as you can and you're not going to make anymore without concession, then is a time to utilize it.

How about a quid pro quo? You scratch my back, I'll scratch yours. That's a lot like compromise. I don't recommend it as the first option. In fact, it might turn out that depending on what the quid pro quo is, you might be actually breaking laws. Be really careful with that tactic.

How about lie, cheat, steal, and manipulate? They'll all get you a deal. Here's the challenge, friends. If you do things that damage relationships, as I said, you've got three domains active here. The **substance,** what's at stake or being considered; the **process,** how they're going to make decisions; and the

relationship. If you do things, if you negotiate, if your process is one that damages the relationship, how do you think things will turn out?

Let's say that you're negotiating with a supplier and you do the hardball routine and you really beat them down on price to a point where maybe they're not even making any money on the deal with you. A year from now, the contract comes up, market conditions have changed. We're not in a recession, there's lots of business out there, and they're looking at the business with you and saying, "I don't want to do this anymore." Are they even going to come back?

What you really need to think about in the way you approach negotiations is that it's really critical to your long-term success. Don't use any of these stupid techniques. Rather negotiate. We want to consider the win-win agreement first, because if you think that a win-lose is the best way to negotiate, I think you're making a classic mistake.

I think this will help illustrate this point. I want you to think about a pendulum in an old grandfather clock. When the pendulum swings from one side to the other, just imagine that second by second by second rotation. When it swings all the way to the right, I want you to imagine that that is the hard-driving bully who negotiates a win-lose agreement. Then it swings past the center point, all the way to the other side. What do you have over there? You've got the wimp who gives concessions and tries to maintain relationships at the expense of the company. Let me ask you something. Which of those positions is the right one? I'd argue that neither one of them is. Often what I hear from managers is they think that if they're not hard charging, they're going to be considered a wimp. They think if they act like they're trying to maintain a relationship, then the other side is going to take advantage of them because they're going to be a bully.

Here's the reality. There is a continuum of positions that we can occupy on that pendulum path. The one that we want is right in the middle where we're maintaining the relationship and getting what we want. Not one or the other. This is not a black or white game, folks. We can create a win-win here.

Burning bridges is a bad plan because if we go for the win-lose, we're going to build resentment, build mistrust, and, as I said earlier, that supplier you beat down on price last year is going to be either a lot harder to deal with this year or he's not going to deal with you at all. I really hope you don't find yourself in a position where he doesn't want to deal with you, especially if it's the only supplier in town because it bought out the competition. Now what is the supplier going to do to you? He's going to make you lose. That's not the right way to look at this.

I want you to think about Fisher and Ury and what they talk about. This is probably the most important point. In negotiations, we take up a position, like it's a conflict, like it's a war. We're going to get behind our castle wall and we're going to defend a position. The reality is that it's not the position that we should be focused on. It should be the interest that leads us to that position.

There's a substantial difference between the position and our interests. The interests are to get at motivation. What is it about that position that's important to us? If we can understand our interests, then what we'll realize is that we can see what the other side is proposing and how those interests align and/or differ from our own.

The Art of Negotiation

We can see the overlap and we can see the contrast in the places where it's not going to work. Here's the real art in negotiating. What's the other party's position? What are their interests behind it? The problem that most people have when they're dealing with another human being is they don't stop to understand the other person's perspective. If you can truly walk a mile in the other person's shoes, if you can truly do that, you can begin to understand their interests.

If you can understand their interests, then perhaps there's a way that you can meet their interests without giving up any of your own. That is a fundamental shift; the paradigm shift in the way that we can approach negotiating that will actually create breakthrough outcomes. It becomes a joint problem-solving technique as opposed to a conflict.

I was once involved in negotiating a significant coaching contract. In negotiating this contract, I was sitting across the conference room table from the general manager. At one point, I looked at him as we were going through the terms of the agreement, and I said, "So and so, is there anything in this contract that could put you in a negative light with your corporate headquarters?" Because he was at a satellite location and it was an interesting culture that wanted facilities to be autonomous but at the same time, if they were too autonomous they would be quickly criticized. He just looked at me like "What?"

Then I realized something really critical and that was that I needed him to know I was looking at this, not from my perspective but from his. I said, "Humor me for a second." I got up out of my chair, I walked around the table, I pulled up the chair next to him, sat down beside him, twisted my chair so I could look him in the eye, and I said, "Let's have another look at the contract and make sure that there is nothing in it that anybody in your corporate office could criticize you for. I don't want this to look negatively for you. If there's anything in the contract that doesn't work for you, let's change it now." It was the most powerful moment because what I was doing was getting so completely into second position, (remember perceptual position from an earlier chapter,) and I was totally looking at this contract from the other person's perspective. Because I was able to do that, he felt even more comfortable doing the deal with me and allowing me to provide coaching to him and his team.

It's important that you learn to understand the other side's interests, not just their position. What are they concerned about? What are their needs? What are their fears? What are their desires that are below their position? Because there are all these things, all these emotions, and all these thoughts driving the position that they're taking. If you can get at those things, then you can actually negotiate from a place of respect and a place of mutual problem solving.

Note that this approach isn't always going to work. Now you're probably thinking, *you just went through all this trouble of explaining how to identify interests and now you're telling us it won't always work. What the heck is going on, Ron?* Look, I want you to recognize that this is Chapter Fifteen, not Chapter One, not Chapter Two. This book is meant to build a solid foundation.

What I have done in each chapter is cover a key skill that you can develop to become an excellent communicator, and by the time we get to Chapter Fifteen, near the end of the book, I need you to recognize that negotiating is one of the most complicated and rewarding forms of communication. I want you to recognize that there are some things that might be barriers that keep others from cooperating with you, even if you get it all right.

Your Reaction Matters

Have you ever noticed that sometimes your facial expression gives you away? I used to deal with a guy in a senior-level position in a company that every time he got upset, he turned red. His head would turn red. You always knew when you were under his skin. If you really wanted to manipulate the guy, you knew how to do it. Not that I ever would, but I'm just telling you.

Your reaction matters. If the other side perceives your reaction as one that is objectionable or distasteful or combative, then all of a sudden, they're going to have some emotional reaction to that. That emotional reaction might be putting up a wall between you and the other person or between them and you. Some other things that can pose barriers are the position that they take. It's obviously different from yours.

You need to understand not just the position but also the interest behind it. How do we actually do that? In Chapter Fourteen, we talked about the power of questions. I gave you several questions. If you go back and look at that list now, some of those questions deal directly with negotiating. I ask, "What's your ideal outcome? What do you need from this negotiation? What's driving your need? If we could create the perfect outcome, what would it be? How would that make you feel?

Questions like that start to get at the interest behind the position. If you are sincerely listening to the other side, if they know that you're listening to them, and if they trust you, they will start to open up and share their interests. Be really careful because the fact that they're going to start opening up and sharing a little bit about what they actually want, meant that now they're starting to get a little bit vulnerable.

If you take advantage of them in that moment, they will never trust you again. Never. In fact, they might never deal with you again. Do not abuse this. This is not a manipulation strategy. This is a way of building trust-based relationships over the long term that both parties win. If they are dissatisfied or they don't trust the way that you're dealing with them, they're not coming back. It will make it increasingly more difficult for you to negotiate deals in the future. I think that's a really key point—the worse you treat people, the harder it will to create win-win outcomes in the future. Remember what motivation speaker Zig Ziglar said, "If you help enough other people get what they want, you'll ultimately get what you want."[30]

The last potential barrier to cooperation is the amount of power, the distribution of power between you and the other party. If you're dealing with employees, they have no power. Just because you have power doesn't mean you should use it. I think you need to develop the ability to influence and negotiate from a place of dignity and respect and mutual success. If you can do that, you will start to create powerful followers who will also develop the ability to lead.

As you develop leaders, how much better do you think your performance can get? That ultimately is the most crucial strategy to be a great manager—the ability to have enough leadership skills yourself that you're building leaders below you.

Breakthrough Strategies

One last thing that I want you to think about when you're in a negotiation and things are not going well. You need to think about how to breakthrough. How do you get past the position? My favorite metaphor for the position problem is two fists just clashing with each other. It's not getting us anywhere and we need to be able to go all the way back to the perceptual position model.

The first strategy is going into second position and understanding things from their point of view and demonstrating to them through the way that you're giving them feedback and paying attention that you are listening to them. You want them to know that you're on their side of the table so that they know they're being listened to, respected, and treated fairly.

Another strategy is to get into third position. Look at the negotiations from a non-emotional point of view from a spectator place. I want you to look at it as if you were a fly on the wall and ask yourself, "What's going on here? What's working, what's not working?

Then come back to one of those powerful questions. What's my role? Be really honest with yourself because it takes two to get into conflict, not one. You do have a role in it, whether you admit it or not. Once you've done that, you've gone into third position and started to look at it from an interested observer point of view, trying to keep your emotions out of it, and seeing what's actually going on.

At this point you can step over to their side and begin to see their point of view and how you can totally reframe the negotiation if you have the relationships in the first place.

Influence vs. Manipulation

One of the most common concerns that comes up when I talk about influencing people or negotiating is the difference between influence and manipulation. It's actually a fundamental difference that we must understand, because it's so easy to cross the line to manipulation. In fact, I would argue that they're almost identical tools in many ways.

If you think about the definition of influence, what is it? Influence is the act or power of producing an effect without an outward exertion of force. Manipulation does the exact same thing. It's just doing it in a way that lacks a certain word and that word is integrity.

One of the ways that I've always looked at the difference between integrity and manipulation is to consider the metaphor of a coin. What's the difference between the head and the tail sides of a coin? If you look at a quarter, specifically the knurled edge around the quarter, if you imagine that wrapped with the word integrity, the difference between influence and manipulation is integrity. Let's go a little deeper because I'm still talking in abstract terms. I want to give you a practical way of knowing when you're influencing things and when you're manipulating them.

It's actually incredibly simple. I want you to reveal your motives to the person you're trying to influence or manipulate. What would happen if you try to influence somebody but you tell them how you're going to interact with them? If you go to somebody and you say I'm collecting money for a cause and what I'm going to do is explain the cause to you and see if it connects with you on an emotional level and, as a result, I'm hoping that you will donate to the cause.

It doesn't take away from my approach to admit that that's what I'm about to do. It either connects with the person or it doesn't. We're not going to feel any worse for the effort. What happens if I try to manipulate a person? "I want to convince you to give me $100. The way I'm going to do it is I'm going to tell you a story about a charity that will tug on your heart strings and make you feel guilty and then you'll give me $100." You see the difference?

The minute manipulators reveal their true motives, the game is up; it's over. They cannot win. Influencers can still achieve the outcome because there's integrity in their approach and in what they're trying to do. It really comes down to one word: transparency. The difference between influencing somebody and manipulating someone is about transparency and integrity. If you're trying to manipulate, you can't reveal your motive. If you're trying to influence, you can.

As it relates to negotiation, I think we need to maintain the same separation that negotiation is partially about influence and it's also a problem-solving activity that's designed to get at the interest of both sides and then use a creative problem-solving technique to find solutions that meet both party's needs.

Let's say you have an employee that you want on a difficult project. That employee is hesitant to get on it. How are you going to approach it? What would you do? If you just play the power card, chances are you're going to get mediocrity at best. The employee will give it an effort but it certainly won't be his best and it might have fear embedded in the base of it.

Let's look at this scenario.

Manager: "Look, I've got this really important project and I've been looking across our entire team and I see that you are exactly the right person for this project. You are prompt, you're well-organized, you're our best problem solver, and you're an excellent communicator. Those skills are exactly what this project needs. Will you do it?"

Employee: "No, sir. I don't want to do it."

Manager: "I want you to do this project, and I see that your position is that you don't want to do it. Help me understand why don't you want to do it. What's behind your saying no right now?"

[If you have a trust-based relationship with this employee, they might tell you this:]

Employee: "This is a really difficult time for my spouse and me.

We are planning on bringing an addition to our family. As a result, I'm concerned that getting involved in a project like this is going to mean a ton of extra hours and those extra hours are going to be taking away from my family responsibility. My job is really important to me. I want to do an excellent job and yet I don't want to let you down. I just don't think I can do this project."

Manager: "What I'm hearing you say, your interests are you want to maintain work-life balance. You want to give a great effort here and want to be recognized as a high performer. Work-life balance is also important to you. You want to make sure that you're home for this addition to your family. By the way, congratulations! That's excellent news. I'm very excited for you. Have you talked to HR about the implications from our benefits point of view?"

Employee: "Yeah, I have."

Manager: "Perfect, just wanted to make sure I took care of that. Let's look at this together. My interest is in helping you progress in your career because I see great things in you. As I said, your communication skills are excellent. You're prompt, you're organized, and you're a great problem solver, the best on our team. I see that there's this one area that if we could get you more skill in, it would open up so many doors for you. That is customer interaction. I really wanted to put you in a place where we could do that. Is that an interest for you? Because that's really where I was trying to come from."

Employee: "I'm so glad you're saying that because that has been an area of struggle for me. I wasn't really sure how to go about it but I do want to get ahead. It's just this is a really difficult time for me."

Manager: "I understand that. What if we designed a solution that allowed you to be on this project to get the experience you need and still find a way to get all your regular duties done so that you perform at the right level? I'm not sure you could get it all done in 8 hours, but I guarantee it won't exceed 10 hours. If you could get home at a decent hour, would that work?"

Employee: "Yeah, that might work."

Manager: "Let's look at your workload right now and see what part of it we might be able to distribute differently or maybe there are some things that you're doing that we could actually eliminate because they're not necessary. Let's do that."

In this particular example, we start to look at how we can negotiate an outcome with an employee. The real key in that exercise is gaining understanding about what your interests are in the first place. What your ideal outcome is. Then understanding the employee's perspective. What is their position? What's driving their position? What are their needs and wants?

Then you can concentrate on finding a solution that allows you to meet both sides. It's really not that difficult to do once you start to dig in and actually listen. In that little example, you also gained some valuable insight into what's important to your employee. Take note of that and do something nice for them (send flowers when the baby arrives). There are so many wins here in this difficult form of communication that can actually help you succeed.

Reflection

1. How can the concepts discussed in this chapter change (for the better) the way you negotiate?

2. Where can you put them into practice?

CHAPTER SIXTEEN

INFLUENCING BEHAVIOR/ PERFORMANCE

In the book, *Theory in Practice: Increasing Professional Effectiveness,* authors Chris Argyris and Donald Schön provide a model of human behavior and the way we learn and interact with the world around us.[32]

Imagine this scenario: You're in a situation and something happens. Maybe there's a quality defect or an employee makes a mistake, a customer calls yelling, the port shuts down and you can't get your trailer in, or a major quality defect occurs. Whatever it is, there's a problem in your business. What do you do? You react. What happens with that reaction is you try to solve the problem. Once the problem is solved, you go back to the status quo and wait until the next problem happens. Then you react and take action. Rinse and repeat.

Argyris and Schön describe this situation as single-loop learning. Basically this is a coping mechanism. When something happens, we come up with a reactionary strategy to address it, and once it's addressed then we go back to the status quo. Obviously we're still doing our job, but for the model's sake, we're waiting for the next problem to occur. If that's all you ever do, what you're going to find is you're just coping with reality.

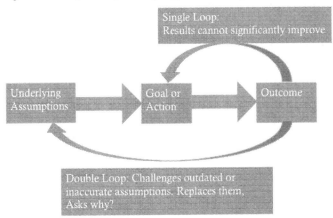

I want to offer you another approach that Argyris and Schön presented. There is a single loop for coping and then there is a double loop, which is really about understanding the process and getting better outcomes.

Imagine you're in a situation and something happens, the customer calls or whatever it is, so you still react. That part of the model never changes. We're managers. We've got to get things done. We've got to know what actions to take in what situations. What I want you to recognize is something I discovered early in my career.

As a professional problem solver, what I found in my first few years in business was that the problems that I was giving excellent solutions to tended to start to creep back in and repeat. I started to ask myself, "Why are these repeating? I gave them the solution." I'd go back to the internal customer and ask them that question and they just kind of looked at me like, "Just solve the problem, Ron." I looked back at them and said, "But I did last time. This is the same problem. Why are you bringing it back to me?" I had reached a dead end because they didn't understand that they needed to change something.

Herein lies the difference between the single and double loop. What we need to do is to challenge our assumptions, our beliefs, our biases, and our mental models about the world around us. What we find is that the way we look at the world is often incomplete and inaccurate. Because of this, we have inaccurate assumptions about the world. If we continue to operate from those inaccurate assumption filters, guess what? When that situation comes up again, we're going to react the exact same way we did last time. You simply can't just repeat what you did last time and expect it to solve your problem.

I had an internal customer come to me (complete with the Chicken Little routine—the sky is falling, the sky is falling) and say, "Ron, we've got this problem. We can't produce any quality product. You've got to solve it. Money's no object. Just basically blank check, whatever you need."

For the next five business days, I pulled my entire problem-solving team from whatever they were working on. This was a major organizational priority. I had them all working on this problem. We were driving down. We were starting to get close to being able to find the root cause, and I remember on the fifth day I went to the representative for the operational unit, and I said, "Here, I need these samples. I need you to stop this production line while it's running and get me these samples." He said, "We can't do that, but I'll see what I can do."

I called him back the next day, "Where are the samples?" Voice mail. The next day, voice mail. A couple days later I got a hold of someone in his office and asked, "Hey, whatever happened to the problem?" The response was these magic words, "The problem went away." I'm thinking *Uh-oh. He's a single-loop learner.* I tried a few more times to get a hold of him, didn't have any luck, but I knew something really powerful that apparently he hadn't quite figured out yet, and that is that if you don't drive to the root cause of the problem, if you don't overcome your inaccurate assumption bias, the problem is coming back, ladies and gentlemen.

Sure enough, about nine months later, he comes to my door again, the same Chicken Little routine, only this time I was ready for him. I said, "Look, dude, here's the deal. You're giving me a blank check, right? Right! Stop the line on production and get me these samples to solve your problem." He said, "I can't do that." I looked at him with all seriousness, and I said, "Then get out of my lab. I can't help you."

He was stunned, absolutely stunned because I wouldn't play the game the way he wanted me to play the game and live in his Chicken Little definition of insanity, his snafu, doing the same thing over and over again. How did it turn out? He went back to his operation and he emergency stopped the production unit as I asked him to do. He brought me the samples I needed, we did the analysis, found the root cause, and we solved the problem. It hasn't been back since. This is a simple and powerful concept.

What's this got to do with your employees and communication? You have assumptions about your employees, don't you? Some of your employees are high performers. Some of them are mediocre. Some of them are low performers. Some of them lack integrity. Some of them aren't smart. You get the point—I could go on and on and on.

What I want you to recognize is that those are biases that you maintain toward those people. They might or might not be accurate. I'm not here to tell you they are or they're not. I've never met your employees. What I am here to tell you is that if you continue to operate from those biases you will communicate to them through those biases and you will not ever get them to get out of the definition of insanity.

In fact, they will live down to your expectations of them. If you think they're not bright, they'll act like they're not bright. If you think they lack integrity, they'll probably find a way to live down to that too. What I want you to recognize is that we need to uncover some of these assumptions that we're making about people and start to replace them with something more accurate.

You may recall in Chapter Thirteen on feedback that I gave you a model and I challenged you to give positive feedback to your lowest-performing employee. I'm coming back to that right now. I'm looking you squarely between the eyes and telling you that this is why you don't see their performance. Maybe they're not performing for you, but I want you to recognize your role in the fact that they're not performing. If you're setting a low expectation for them without even realizing it because you've made assumptions about them, you talk down to them in such a way that they don't understand how to perform at a higher level, and they're not inspired to get there for you, guess what? You get what you pay for. You get what you invest in.

What I want you to do is uncover that assumption, challenge it, and go to that employee and treat him or her differently. See them for their best rather than their worst. See them for a realistic best, something that they could achieve. If you think they're not bright, then just up it a little bit. Give them a task that's a little bit beyond their comfort zone or their ability level and see if they can't pull it off. Human beings are incredibly resilient and I think you'll find that they want to grow, but they want to grow in ways that are honoring to you if they respect you. The key is they've got to respect you. You've got to earn that, and then you've got to challenge them to grow.

This is a really, really powerful model as it relates to the subtleties of communication. I challenge you to start to think about a thought in your head as you start to encounter an employee. What's the first picture that comes to your mind's eye as you see each employee? Maybe even write it down. Be careful that the employees can't find it, but write it down and ask yourself, "Is this accurate? Has this in any way limited my ability to help this employee perform?"

I truly believe the snafu principle, like the definition of insanity—doing the same thing over and over again and expecting a different result—is largely based on this model. The good news is that you can overcome the assumptions that you've made about people by finding them, changing them, and giving your employees hope of a better future with your ability to see them for what they are realistically best at.

Reflection

1. What do you need to start questioning about the way you interact with those around you?

2. How do you ensure you are learning every day how to look beyond your reactionary instinctive coping (single loop) mechanisms?

3. Now that you have completed this book, what steps will you take to overcome your snafus?

Epilogue

I left the last page intentionally blank, as I am symbolically listening to you.

So what did you learn?

How has this book affected you?

Are you ready to go further, and overcome your communication snafus?

info@thesnafuprinciple.com

References

1. http://www.businessperform.com/workplace-communication/poor-communication-costs.html

2. http://www.holmesreport.com/latest/article/the-cost-of-poor- communications

3. http://employeeengagement.com/wp- content/uploads/2013/06/Gallup-2013-State-of-the-American- Workplace-Report.pdf

4. http://www.ncbi.nlm.nih.gov/pmc/articles/PMC1765783/pdf/v 013p00i85.pdf

5. http://www.instituteforpr.org/organizational-communication- and -financial-performance/

6. http://blogs.wsj.com/economics/2015/01/29/for-many-u-s- families -financial-disaster-is-just-one-setback-away/

7. http://en.wikipedia.org/wiki/DISC_assessment.

8. Navarro, Joe, and Marvin Karlins. (2008). *What Every BODY Is Saying: An Ex-FBI Agents guide to speed reading people:* New York, New York: Collins Living.

9. Goleman, Daniel, Richard E. Boyatzis, and Annie McKee. (2002). *Primal Leadership: Realizing the Power of Emotional Intelligence.* Boston, Massachusetts: Harvard Business School.

10. Northouse, Peter Guy. (2013). *Leadership: Theory and Practice.* Thousand Oaks, California: SAGE. 164.

11. McKay, Matthew, Martha Davis, and Patrick Fanning. (1995) *Messages: The Communication Skills Book.* Oakland, California: New Harbinger Publications.

12. http://theartofcharm.com/podcast-episodes/julian-treasure- conscious -listening-episode-320/

13. Adapted from Hamilton, Cheryl. (2005). *Communicating for Results: A Guide for Business and the Professions* Belmont, California: Thomson/Wadsworth. 5.

14. Cashman, Kevin. (2008). *Leadership from the Inside Out: Becoming a Leader for Life.* San Francisco, California: Berrett-Koehler Publishers.

15. http://www.speaking.pitt.edu/student/public- speaking/basics.html and also Hamilton. *Communicating for Results: A Guide for Business and the Professions.*

16. http://www.mindtools.com/CommSkll/ActiveListening.htm. See also Davis, Martha, Kim Paleg, and Patrick Fanning. (2004). *The Messages Workbook: Powerful Strategies for Effective Communication at Work & Home.* Oakland, California: New Harbinger Publications.

17. Greenberg, Jerald, and Robert A. Baron. (2010). *Behavior in Organizations.* Upper Saddle River, New Jersey: Pearson Education.

18. http://www.apa.org/monitor/oct05/mirror.aspx

19. Goulston, Mark. (2009). *Just Listen: Discover the Secret to Getting through to Absolutely Anyone.* New York, New York: AMACOM.

20. http://www.businessballs.com/freeteambuildingactivities.htm

21. https://books.google.com/books?id=YAUnLY2KnewC&pg=PA134&lpg=PA134&dq=ken+blanchard+manager+expectations+survey+results&source=bl&ots=7CdrFs6QNm&sig=AtAFE27NRXIS5D9-m7BWARY7Zc4&hl=en&sa=X&ei=oTZeVb2NA46qogTtrYDYCw&ved=0CCMQ6AEwATgK#v=onepage&q=ken%20blanc hard%20manager%20expectations%20survey%20results&f=false)

22. http://www.kenblanchard.com/getattachment/Leading- Research/Research/Ten-Performance-Management-Process- Gaps/Employee-Work-Passion-Vol-7-MK0795.pdf

23. http://home.ncifcrf.gov/SAICFTraining/2011_Gallup_Questions.pdf

24. http://www.gordontraining.com/free-workplace- articles/learning-a-new-skill-is-easier-said-than-done/

25. Weitzel, Sloan R. (2000). *Feedback That Works: How to Build and Deliver Your Message*. San Diego, California, CCL.

26. Horstman, Mark. http://manager-tools.com.

27. Covey, Stephen. (2013). *The Seven Habits of Highly Effective People*. New York, New York: Simon & Schuster.

28. Hurst, Ron. (2014). *The First Questions: Coaching Your Way to Leadership Success*. Lulu Publishing Services.

29. Fisher, Roger, and William Ury. (2011). *Getting to Yes: Negotiating Agreement without Giving In*. New York, New York: Penguin Books.

30. http://www.karrass.com

31. http://www.ziglar.com/quotes/you-can-have-everything-life- you-want

32. Argyris, Chris, and Schön, Donald. (1992). *Theory in Practice: Increasing Professional Effectiveness*. New York, New York: Jossey-Bass.

Acknowledgments

This book is inspired by the hundreds of trainees, past and present, who have labored with me to build outstanding communications training programs. Each course improved and changed because of your feedback. You have helped me to find my voice and listen more deeply.

To the professors at Fielding Graduate University Evidence Based Coaching program, my sincerest and most heartfelt thanks for teaching me how to really listen.

To countless authors and colleagues whose advice I have sought and employed in developing my communication abilities, I thank you.

Finally to Best Seller Publishing, a thank you in advance for helping make this project a great success.

Made in the USA
San Bernardino, CA
25 January 2019